ONE

ONE

ELENA SILCOCK

HAMLYN

First published in Great Britain in 2021 by Hamlyn, an imprint of
Octopus Publishing Group Ltd
Carmelite House
50 Victoria Embankment
London EC4Y 0DZ
www.octopusbooks.co.uk

An Hachette UK Company
www.octopusbooks.co.uk
www.octopusbooksusa.com

Distributed in the US by
Hachette Book Group
1290 Avenue of the Americas
4th and 5th Floors
New York, NY 10104

Distributed in Canada by
Canadian Manda Group
664 Annette St
Toronto, Ontario, Canada M6S 2C8

ISBN 978 0 600 63704 2 (UK)
ISBN 978 0 600 63709 7 (US)

A CIP catalogue record for this book is available from the British Library.

Printed and bound in China

10 9 8 7 6 5 4 3 2 1

Commissioning Editor Louise McKeever
Art Director Yasia Williams
Designer Peter Dawson, Grade Design
Senior Editor Alex Stetter
Photographer Louise Hagger
Props Stylist Alexander Breeze
Production Manager Caroline Alberti

CONTENTS

INTRODUCTION

Throughout my cooking and writing career – and in that, I include my teenage years of throwing a lot of things in pans to feed my hungry brothers – I've always known that, in reality, low-maintenance cooking is where it's at. Fancy and fussy food has its place gracing the tables of high-end restaurants, but when it comes to cooking at home, I base my recipes around a few key ideas:

I DON'T WANT TO HAVE TO WASH UP MORE THAN ABSOLUTELY NECESSARY (OR AT ALL, IF I CAN HELP IT!)

I try to use minimal tools and dishes, to serve straight out of the pan at the table and (preferably) to establish the rule that the cook doesn't wash up after dinner. These are all tricks that I keep up my sleeve to minimize time spent in rubber gloves.

I DON'T WANT TO BE STRESSED

At its best, cooking should be fun. At the very least, it should not be a source of stress. I try to cook recipes that don't require endless steps, that use handy shortcuts (I won't be soaking beans overnight any time soon) and that don't need much re-reading to churn out again at speed if someone comes over for a last-minute dinner. I'm also a lot less likely to forget something in the oven when it's all in one pan on the stove top in front of me!

I DON'T WANT TO USE A WHOLE CUPBOARD OF INGREDIENTS

I don't think recipes need to have tons of different flavours to be delicious. I use flavours that work together, and I use them sparingly. I try to use good-quality ingredients, which in reality do all the hard work for you.

I DON'T WANT TO HAVE TO BUY LOTS OF INGREDIENTS

There are two ways to avoid having to run out to pick up lots of missing ingredients every time you cook. First, focus on your store-cupboard favourites. Having olive oil, garlic, ginger and lemon around usually at least halves the shopping list, and a few key spices like cumin seeds, ground coriander, fennel seeds and turmeric will generally mean that all you need to do is nip out for some fresh produce when trying a new recipe – and that's the fun bit.

Secondly, figure out substitutions. Learning to substitute is by far the most valuable lesson I've learned in a kitchen. Swap in and swap out – see pages 15–16 for some suggestions – when you're stuck!

I WANT EVERYONE AT THE TABLE TO BE SATISFIED (AND IMPRESSED)
Portions should be big enough to satisfy, and hopefully anyone eating the food should have enjoyed it so much that they offer to do the washing up.

All these factors played a part in the creation of this book. Cooking in one pan makes the cooking experience so much easier and suits all kitchen sizes. It minimizes washing up and it also ensures that all your flavours are sealed in one place. It makes cooking less daunting, less stressful and more manageable. It's how everyone *really* wants to cook. My hope is that, as well as being easy to follow, the recipes in this book will surprise you with just how impressive a one-pan meal can be.

KEY TO SYMBOLS

 FRYING PAN

 SAUCEPAN

 SERVES (4)

 TIME (45 MINS)

 VEGETARIAN

 VEGAN

PICK A PAN

I use two kinds of pan in this book: a large frying pan and a large saucepan.

THE FRYING PAN
A large non-stick, high-sided frying pan with a lid

Get a big pan, at least 28cm (11in) in diameter. This size will work when you're cooking for one and when you're cooking for four. Things will crisp up when they need to crisp up, and you won't be endlessly trying to turn greens so they each get their turn at the base of the pan.

Make sure it's non-stick. Trust me on this. One-pan cooking is great, but scraping the base of a pan coated in a layer of your lovingly prepared meal is not.

High sides are best. You don't want precious ingredients spilling out all over the stove top.

It needs a cover. You can improvise with a baking sheet, but if your frying pan has a lid, it will make your life much easier.

THE SAUCEPAN
A large saucepan or casserole dish with a lid

Get a large saucepan. It's best if you can fit a whole bag of pasta in there without having to stir too much. Even if you're cooking smaller portions, having a bigger pan gives everything a bit more room and makes it much easier to stir, especially when adding handfuls of greens to wilt down!

Choose one with a lid. For most of the saucepan recipes, you'll need to cover the filling at some point. Again, you can improvise with a baking sheet, but make sure you have something you can use to weigh it down. I often add a layer of tin foil under the lid if I'm slow-cooking meat: this adds an extra seal and makes sure no steam escapes.

HOW TO GET THE BEST OUT OF ONE-PAN COOKING

Now that you're cooking with one pan, here are a few tips and tricks to make the most of this low-maintenance style:

1 > Grate garlic and ginger directly into the pan when you're using them: it saves on time. You can usually do this with Parmesan as well. A microplane is a handy piece of kit to have at the ready to minimize the amount of chopping you're doing. You can also crush garlic straight into the pan, without peeling it before you put it in the garlic press.

2 > Don't bother peeling things like carrots or potatoes: just give them a quick wash. Peeling is a waste of time anyway, as so much of the flavour is in the skin! Peeling ginger is also unnecessary; just grate it straight away.

3 > Use your kitchen scales to measure your liquids as well as dry ingredients – for most liquid ingredients, a gram and a millilitre will be the same, or almost the same (it blew my mind to discover this!). This saves you time and washing up, and often means you can combine ingredients as you're weighing them.

4 > Always have lemons and limes on hand. Many recipes use citrus at the end, and it's a great way to add a kick of freshness to something that's been cooking away in a pot. Lemon or lime juice will usually do the trick, and serving extra wedges at the table is also a great way to let people add a little zing of their own before eating.

5 > A few toppings go a long way when it comes to flavour! A lot of these recipes are topped with flavoured yogurts, quick herby dressings or scatterings of nuts and seeds. They're the key to making sure the dish really impresses: they either freshen, cool or add a crunch.

6 > Serve straight to the table. Gone are the days of fancy plating. Just put the pan on the table and let people serve themselves, putting on their own toppings and garnishes for an insta-ready dinner.

TRICKS AND FIXES

If your dish isn't tasting quite right or feels like it's lacking a little something, don't worry. It happens, even with the best recipes. When I have a dish that's not quite *there*, I have a couple of fail-safe fixes on standby.

SEASONING
Salt, salt, salt – in everything! Taste regularly as you're cooking – things can usually take more seasoning than you may have initially thought.

OLIVE OIL
Add a bit more olive oil. My measurements for olive oil are estimates only – a splash more here and there can give that extra bit of oomph if you think the flavour needs to be a bit richer.

SUGAR
Sometimes even the most savoury of dishes just need a pinch of sugar to round them.

LEMONS, LIMES AND VINEGAR
Sometimes you just need a little more acidity. Some lemons and limes are juicier than others, so taste as you add and feel free to add a bit more if you think it's needed.

STOCK CUBE
Some stock cubes are more flavoursome than others. If you've used the right amount of stock in a dish but it's tasting a bit bland, crumble a little more of a stock cube in there to give it an extra flavour kick.

ANCHOVIES
People can be afraid of anchovies and I get it: on their own, they can be a bit much. However, in fish dishes they're the perfect seasoning – salty, with a bit more depth. Add four or five to the pan and watch them disintegrate, mingling with the other ingredients to make your dish taste INCREDIBLE.

COOK IT FOR A LITTLE LONGER
Sometimes all it needs is a little more time. If a dish seems a bit too loose or watery, simply let the pan bubble away for a little longer, until the sauce thickens. The same rule applies if your slow-cooking meat is still a bit tough: just replace the lid and let it bubble for a bit longer. It'll be meltingly tender in another half hour or so.

STORE CUPBOARD

No one likes piling a shopping trolley full of ingredients for one dish and the key to avoiding this is a pantry well-stocked with a few staples. For the recipes in this book, having the items listed below already on hand will halve your shopping list. I also try to reuse spices and store-cupboard ingredients in different recipes, so you won't find yourself buying an ingredient and then having no other use for it.

FRESH INGREDIENTS TO KEEP AROUND
Garlic
Ginger
Red and green chillies
Lemons and limes

IN MY CUPBOARD
Olive oil (you can sub in other oils if you need to, but olive oil is the most-used ingredient in my kitchen)
Soy sauce
Honey
Sesame oil
Anchovies
Stock cubes
Red and white wine (I tend to cook with something I don't mind drinking, so nothing gets wasted!)

ON MY SPICE RACK
Fennel seeds
Dried chilli flakes
Cumin seeds (or ground cumin)
Ground coriander
Turmeric
Garam masala
Cinnamon

Other spices come in handy, but these provide the real backbone to many of the recipes in this book.

OTHER KITCHEN TOOLS

This book is about low-maintenance cooking, and I really believe you don't need cupboards stuffed with utensils to make amazing food. Here are the few things that are pretty essential, as well as a few that are handy – with substitution options!

A decent knife. Make sure it's sharp. You really only need one knife, plus a bread knife if you're cutting loaves.

A chopping board. Please not a glass one or one that slides around your surface while you're chopping!

A fine grater or microplane. This is my favourite tool, perfect for the speedy grating of garlic and ginger directly into the pan!

A silicone spatula or wooden spoon. I prefer the spatula because nothing gets wasted when you use it to scrape everything out of the pan.

A few mixing bowls. Plus a few nice small bowls to serve any toppings in.

A few spoons. Teaspoons, tablespoons and serving spoons. For measuring, for stirring, for tasting, for serving.

A whisk. You can use a fork if you don't have a whisk, but sometimes it can really come in handy.

Scales. As much as I don't think you need to worry too much about weighing everything to the exact gram, a good set of kitchen scales is great to have around.

A mini chopper. This isn't 100 per cent necessary, but it's a real secret weapon in the kitchen, saving on time and arduous chopping.

HOW TO SUBSTITUTE

Understanding how to substitute is the best lesson you can learn in the kitchen. It means that so many recipes become available to you and ensures you waste as little from your fridge as possible. I've tried to offer substitutes in the recipe tips throughout, but here are some guidelines to get you started.

OLIVE OIL
Use alternative oils, such as sunflower, vegetable, rapeseed, sesame or coconut. The flavour will change a little, especially if using sesame oil, but they'll all do the trick! You can also swap oil for butter, but remember that it burns a little faster.

LEMON JUICE
Swap for lime juice or vinegar. You're looking for something that will add a hint of acidity, so use whatever you have.

ONIONS
Replace with spring onions, celery, leeks or fennel – all will work, while providing a slightly different flavour.

GREENS
Whenever I use greens in this book, they can be swapped and substituted. Leafy greens, such as such as kale, spring greens and spinach, can easily be swapped for each other, and you can substitute firm greens like broccoli or sugar snap peas for other firm greens, such as green beans or mangetout.

FISH
White fish, such as hake, can be swapped for another white fish option, such as cod or seabass. Just look at the thickness of the fish and adjust the cooking time where needed.

SLOW-COOKING MEATS
You can replace one kind of slow-cooking meat with another slow-cooking cut from another animal: use beef shin rather than lamb shoulder, or pork shoulder rather than beef cheeks. The flavour will be different, but the cooking instructions and timing will be pretty much the same.

SPICES

These are a little trickier, as it's hard to substitute something with a distinctive flavour easily for another, but follow your nose. If you don't have some of the spices you need, you can play around a little and add something else instead – you might create something new and great! If you have some, but not all, of the spices listed in a recipe, another option is just to use the ones that you do have, but up the quantity a little.

PULSES

Canned pulses can be swapped for other canned pulses, although if you're swapping white beans for something like kidney beans, just be aware that the dish will look very different!

RICE OR GRAINS

Replace rice pouches with pouches of other cooked grains, using brown rice if you'd rather, or mixed grains and lentils. If you want to swap around dry grains, be aware that some have longer cooking times than others. For example, brown rice takes substantially longer to cook than white rice, so make sure you alter the recipe accordingly.

1

THAT LITTLE BIT LIGHTER

HAKE, ARTICHOKE AND CARAMELIZED FENNEL
WITH BROWN RICE AND LEMON

This can be both a speedy midweek dinner and a dish to show off in front of friends and family. It sounds fancy, but it really just makes the most of some of my favourite cheat items. If you can get your hands on some hake with the skin on, use it! If not, simply skip the first step.

4 hake fillets, about 225 g (8 oz) each

2 tablespoons olive oil

2 fennel bulbs, halved lengthways, then cut into wedges

1 garlic clove, grated or crushed

2 teaspoons fennel seeds

125 ml (4 fl oz) white wine

2 x 250 g (9 oz) pouches ready-cooked brown or wholegrain rice

small bunch of fresh dill or flat-leaf parsley, roughly chopped

180 g (6½ oz) chargrilled artichokes, roughly chopped

1 lemon, halved

sea salt and freshly ground black pepper

1 > If your hake has its skin on, heat a large non-stick, high-sided frying pan over a high heat. Rub the hake skin with 1 tablespoon olive oil and season with salt. Once the frying pan is hot, place the hake into the pan, skin-side down, and cook for 2–3 minutes, until the skin is crisp. Remove from the pan and set aside on a plate.

2 > Heat 1 tablespoon olive oil in the frying pan over a medium–high heat. Add the fennel wedges along with a big pinch of salt. Fry for around 10 minutes, turning regularly, until the fennel is starting to turn golden. Add the garlic and fennel seeds and fry for 2 minutes more. Pour in the wine, along with 300 ml (10 fl oz) water, and bring to the boil. Cook for 5 minutes, until the fennel has totally softened.

3 > Add the rice, half the dill or parsley, and the chopped artichokes. Squeeze in the juice of half a lemon and season well with salt and pepper. Stir to combine and reduce the heat to low. Snuggle the hake into the rice, skin-side up. Cook for around 4–5 minutes, or until the fish is flaking apart.

4 > Scatter over the remaining herbs and serve with the remaining lemon half to squeeze over at the table.

CHUNKY MEXICAN TOMATO SOUP
WITH FRIED TORTILLAS

The key to any good tomato soup is letting the tomatoes cook for long enough to sweeten so that the soup tastes rich; they need a good 15 minutes. If you don't like spice, omit the chipotle paste or chilli flakes and just use 1 teaspoon smoked paprika.

2 tablespoons olive oil

2 corn or wheat tortillas

1 large red onion, finely chopped

1 garlic clove, grated

1 teaspoon ground coriander

½ teaspoon cumin seeds

1 tablespoon chipotle paste
    (or 1 teaspoon chilli flakes and
    1 teaspoon smoked paprika)

400 g (14 oz) can whole cherry
    tomatoes or chopped
    tomatoes

1 vegetable stock cube

400 g (14 oz) can black beans,
    drained and rinsed

200 g (7 oz) can sweetcorn,
    drained and rinsed

1 lime, ½ juiced and ½ cut into
    wedges

1 avocado, peeled, stoned and
    cubed

sea salt and freshly ground black
    pepper

To serve
soured cream
freshly chopped coriander

1 > Heat 1 tablespoon of the olive oil in a large saucepan over a high heat. Use scissors to snip the tortillas in half, then into strips. Scatter into the pan and fry for 2 minutes until crisp. Set aside on a plate lined with kitchen roll to drain.

2 > Heat the remaining olive oil in the pan over a medium–high heat. Add the onion with a pinch of salt and cook for 3–4 minutes, until softened.

3 > Stir in the garlic, along with the ground coriander, cumin seeds and chipotle paste. Cook for 2 more minutes, then tip in the can of tomatoes. Refill the emptied can with hot water twice and pour that into the pan, too. Crumble in the stock cube and stir. Bring to the boil, then reduce the heat to a simmer and bubble away for 15–20 minutes.

4 > Add the black beans and sweetcorn to the soup. Season well with salt and pepper and squeeze in the lime juice.

5 > Divide the soup between 2 bowls and add a dollop of soured cream and some chopped avocado to each. Scatter over the tortilla chips and coriander, and serve with the lime wedges.

GREEN LENTIL MINESTRONE
WITH SPRING GREENS AND PARMESAN SPRINKLE

This is inspired by a spring minestrone my best mate made for me on a really sunny April day. I ate the same soup for three consecutive days and was still sad when the batch was over. Skip the pancetta if you want to make it veggie, and swap out the spring greens for whatever greens you like: asparagus, spinach or broccoli are all great in this.

1 tablespoon olive oil

160 g (5¾ oz) diced pancetta (optional)

3 garlic cloves, finely sliced

1.5 litres (2¾ pints) vegetable or chicken stock

25 g (1 oz) Parmesan cheese, grated, plus the rind (this thickens the soup)

400 g (14 oz) can green lentils

200 g (7 oz) dried pasta, such as short rigatoni or fusilli

small bunch of fresh flat-leaf parsley, roughly chopped

small bunch of fresh mint, roughly chopped

zest and juice of 1 unwaxed lemon

2 tablespoons toasted hazelnuts, roughly chopped

200 g (7 oz) spring greens or cabbage, finely sliced

200 g (7 oz) frozen peas or broad beans

sea salt and freshly ground black pepper

1 > Heat the olive oil in a large non-stick saucepan over a medium–high heat. Add the diced pancetta, if using, and fry for about 5 minutes, until crispy.

2 > Reduce the heat to medium and add the garlic slices. Gently fry for about 2 minutes until they begin to turn golden. Tip the stock into the pan, along with the Parmesan rind. Add the whole can of green lentils, along with their liquid. Increase the heat to medium–high and bring to the boil. Season with salt, then add the pasta and boil away for 10 minutes.

3 > Meanwhile, make the Parmesan sprinkle. Place half the parsley and mint in a bowl and set the rest aside. Add the grated Parmesan, lemon zest and hazelnuts to the herbs in the bowl and stir to combine. Season well.

4 > Once the pasta is cooked through, stir in the spring greens and peas or broad beans. Cook until the greens are just wilted, then squeeze in the lemon juice and stir through the remaining herbs. Bring to the boil.

5 > Remove and discard the Parmesan rind, then ladle the minestrone into 4 bowls, scatter over the Parmesan sprinkle and serve.

THAI CHICKEN NOODLE SOUP

Chicken noodle soup comes in all shapes and sizes, but this is one of my favourites. Slurp away, people: it's the only way to really enjoy this kind of dish.

1 tablespoon sesame oil

small bunch of spring onions, sliced

1 garlic clove, grated

thumb-sized piece of fresh root ginger, grated

3–4 tablespoons Thai green curry paste (depending on the strength of the paste)

400 ml (14 fl oz) can coconut milk

1 chicken stock cube

2 large chicken breasts, about 180 g (6½ oz) each

1 tablespoon peanut butter

200 g (7 oz) green beans, cut into 3 cm (1¼ inch) lengths

200 g/7 oz dried rice noodles

1 lime, ½ juiced and ½ cut into wedges

1 tablespoon soy sauce

sea salt and freshly ground black pepper

To serve

handful of roasted peanuts, roughly chopped

freshly chopped coriander

1 > Heat the sesame oil in a large saucepan over a medium–high heat. Add the spring onions, garlic and ginger. Fry for a couple of minutes, then add the curry paste. Fry for 2 minutes further, then pour in the coconut milk. Refill the emptied can with water twice and pour that into the pan too. Bring to the boil and add the stock cube, stirring well to make sure it dissolves.

2 > Reduce the heat right down to low, so the soup is just simmering. Season the chicken breasts, then add them to the pan. Cover with a lid and simmer for 15 minutes – make sure not to boil the soup, as this will make the chicken tough!

3 > Lift the chicken breasts out of the pan and set aside on a plate or board. Increase the heat to medium–high, add the peanut butter, green beans and noodles to the pan and bubble for 5 minutes, until the beans are bright green and just tender and the noodles are cooked through. Meanwhile, use two forks to shred the chicken breasts. Add the lime juice and soy sauce to the pan and season to taste. If the soup looks a little thick, add a splash of water.

4 > Remove from the heat and stir the shredded chicken into the soup.

5 > Divide the soup between 4 bowls, and top with the chopped peanuts and fresh coriander. Serve with the lime wedges for squeezing over at the table.

SPRING POACHED CHICKEN
WITH SPEEDY PESTO

This recipe is springtime in a bowl. It's half comforting and half refreshing, ideal for when you're too hot for a winter stew and too cold for a summer salad. If you don't want to make the speedy pesto sauce, just serve this scattered with the reserved parsley and a dollop of store-bought pesto. PS Please don't boil your chicken instead of simmering it gently; it'll become super tough and you'll regret it, I promise.

450 g (1 lb) baby potatoes, halved

300 g (10½ oz) baby carrots, halved lengthways

2 bay leaves

3 garlic cloves, left whole

2 chicken stock cubes

small bunch of fresh flat-leaf parsley

4 skinless and boneless chicken breasts, about 165 g (5¾ oz) each

200 g (7 oz) frozen peas

200 g (7 oz) asparagus spears, sliced into 3 cm (1¼ in) lengths

200 g (7 oz) spring greens

4 tablespoons crème fraîche

sea salt and freshly ground black pepper

For the speedy pesto (optional)

reserved parsley (see above)

juice of 1 lemon

60 ml (4 tablespoons) olive oil

2 tablespoons walnuts, toasted

1 > Tip the potatoes and carrots into a large saucepan. Cover with 1 litre (1¾ pints) cold water and a big pinch of salt. Add the bay leaves, whole garlic cloves and the stock cubes. Add a handful of parsley (saving the rest for the pesto). Place the saucepan over a high heat and bring to the boil, then reduce the heat to low: it should be gently bubbling. Add the chicken breasts, cover with a lid and simmer for 15 minutes.

2 > Meanwhile, make the pesto sauce, if using. In a small food processor, blitz the remaining parsley with the lemon juice, olive oil and walnuts. Season with salt and pepper and set aside.

3 > Remove the lid from the saucepan and scoop out the garlic cloves with a slotted spoon. Add the peas, asparagus and spring greens. Increase the heat and quickly bring to the boil, then immediately remove from the heat: this will make sure that the dish is hot and the veg is cooked, but the chicken isn't overcooked.

4 > Spoon into 4 bowls, adding a chicken breast to each bowl to start with, then spooning over the veg. Add a dollop of crème fraîche and some pesto to each bowl. Season with salt and pepper and serve.

SWEETCORN AND POTATO FRITTERS
WITH CURRY YOGURT

If a sweetcorn fritter and a potato rosti had a baby, it would look a little something like this. The curry yogurt is an ideal topping and the salsa is highly recommended, but not essential if you're in a bit of a rush or don't fancy the extra washing up!

250 g (9 oz) potatoes, coarsely grated

200g (7 oz) can sweetcorn

1 egg

2 tablespoons self-raising flour

½ small bunch of spring onions, finely sliced

pinch of dried red chilli flakes

1 tablespoon salted butter or olive oil

sea salt and freshly ground black pepper

½ small bunch of fresh mint or coriander, leaves picked, to serve

For the yogurt

150 ml (5 fl oz) natural yogurt

½ tablespoon mild curry powder

juice and zest of ½ lime

For the side salad (optional)

1 avocado, peeled and cubed

½ cucumber, cubed

juice of ½ lime

1 tablespoon olive oil

½ small bunch of spring onions, finely sliced

½ small bunch of fresh mint or coriander, leaves picked

1 > Lay out a clean tea towel on the work surface. Tip the grated potato into the tea towel and draw the corners in to create a little bag. Twist the bag so all the grated potato is tightly packed. Holding the tea towel over a sink, squeeze it as tightly as you can until all the water has come out.

2 > Tip the grated potato into a bowl. Add the sweetcorn, egg, self-raising flour, spring onions and chilli flakes. Season with plenty of salt and pepper and mix well. Use your hands to squeeze the mixture into 6 balls.

3 > To make the curry yogurt, mix together the yogurt, curry powder and lime juice and zest in a small bowl. Season well with salt and pepper. If making the side salad, place all the ingredients in a salad bowl and toss to combine. Season well with salt and pepper and set aside.

4 > Heat around half a tablespoon butter or olive oil in a large non-stick frying pan over a medium–high heat. Add 2 of the potato and sweetcorn balls, then use a spatula to flatten them out into fritters around 8 cm (3¼ inches) in diameter. Fry for 2 minutes on each side until golden and cooked through. Set the fritters aside on a plate and repeat with the remaining ½ tablespoon butter or olive oil and the other 2 potato and sweetcorn balls.

5 > Serve 2 fritters per person with a big dollop of the yogurt on each plate. Scatter over the mint or coriander leaves and serve with the salad on the side, if you like.

Photograph overleaf >

MISO SALMON AND SESAME GREENS

Miso is a Japanese ingredient that has become a household favourite. It's salty, but also offers much more complexity than a pinch of sea salt. In this dish, it makes a simple fillet of salmon sing. I've paired the miso salmon with sesame greens, because they really are a magical way to power towards your 5-a-day. Serve with noodles or a pouch of rice if you want to make it a little more substantial.

2 tablespoons sesame seeds

2 salmon fillets, skin on, about 125 g (4¼ oz) each

1 tablespoon sesame, vegetable or olive oil

bunch of spring onions, three-quarters sliced into 3 cm (1¼ inch) lengths, the rest finely sliced

200 g (7 oz) green beans sliced into 3 cm (1¼ inch) lengths

1 garlic clove, grated

thumb-sized piece of fresh root ginger, grated

300 g (10½ oz) spinach, kale or spring greens, finely sliced

sea salt and freshly ground black pepper

½ lime, cut into wedges, to serve

For the miso dressing

½ tablespoon white miso paste

1 teaspoon clear honey or a pinch of brown sugar

juice of ½ lime

½ tablespoon soy sauce

1 > Place the sesame seeds on a plate and spread them out thinly. Dip the salmon fillets, skin-side down, into the sesame seeds, creating a light layer of seeds on the skin. Place the salmon, seeded-skin-side down, in a cold non-stick frying pan. If there are any seeds left on the plate, set them aside for later.

2 > Set the frying pan containing the salmon over a medium heat and cook for 10 minutes, until the skin is crisp and the sesame seeds are golden.

3 > While the salmon is cooking, prepare the dressing. In a small bowl or jar, mix together the dressing ingredients along with 1 tablespoon water. Season well and set aside.

4 > When the salmon is cooked, remove it from the pan and set it aside on another plate, skin-side up. Keeping the pan on the heat, increase the heat to medium–high and add the oil. Once it's hot, add the spring onion and green bean lengths, along with any remaining sesame seeds. Fry for a couple of minutes, then add the garlic and ginger and fry for 1 minute further. Add the leafy greens (it looks like a lot but will wilt down) and toss really well. Cook for around 3 minutes, stirring, until the vegetables are bright green and any water has evaporated.

5 > Remove from the heat and stir the dressing into the mixture in the pan. Spread the vegetables out into an even layer across the pan, then create 2 spaces and tuck the salmon fillets in, skin-side up. Return the pan to the heat and cook for 2 minutes, until the salmon is cooked through and flakes when prodded. Scatter over the spring onion slices and serve with the lime wedges.

WINTER BEAN AND CAVOLO NERO SOUP

Soup to soothe on a cold – and probably rainy – winter's day. If you've got some garlic bread, it wouldn't go amiss on the side.

1 tablespoon olive oil

3 carrots, peeled, quartered lengthways and chopped into 1 cm (½ in) chunks

3 celery sticks, finely sliced

2 garlic cloves, sliced

small bunch of fresh flat-leaf parsley, roughly chopped

1 tablespoon tomato puree

400 g (14 oz) can butter beans, drained

400 g (14 oz) can cannellini beans

1 stock cube (vegetable or chicken)

25 g (1 oz) Parmesan cheese, grated, plus the rind if you can

200 g (7 oz) cavolo nero, woody stems removed, leaves roughly chopped

juice of 1 lemon

sea salt and freshly ground black pepper

toasted pine nuts, to serve

1 > Heat the olive oil in a large saucepan over a medium heat. Add the carrots, celery and garlic, along with most of the parsley. Stir well and gently fry for around 10 minutes, so everything softens, but doesn't colour too much.

2 > Stir the tomato puree into the pan, making sure it coats all the veggies. Cook for around 1 minute, then tip the drained butter beans into the pan. Now add the whole can of cannellini beans, including the liquid from the can. Refill one of the emptied cans with water and pour that into the pan too. Add the stock cube, and Parmesan rind, if using. Bring to the boil and let it bubble for 5 minutes.

3 > Now add the cavolo nero to the pan. Let it wilt into the soup for a couple of minutes, then add half the lemon juice and a handful of the grated Parmesan. Season well with salt and pepper.

4 > Remove and discard the Parmesan rind (if used), then spoon the soup into 4 bowls. Top with the remaining grated Parmesan, another squeeze of lemon, the remaining parsley and the pine nuts.

SMOKY SQUASH SOUP
WITH ROASTED ALMONDS

I love making this with smoked almonds, as they give it such a distinct, smoky flavour. However, it's equally tasty with plain roasted almonds, which are usually a little easier to get hold of. If your roasted almonds are unsmoked and unsalted, you'll need to add a little more seasoning.

1 tablespoon olive oil

1 onion, sliced

1 garlic clove, grated

2 teaspoons paprika (use hot paprika if you like spice)

1 large butternut squash (around 1 kg/2 lb 4 oz), peeled, halved, deseeded and chopped into 3 cm (1¼ inch) chunks

75 g (2½ oz) smoked almonds or roasted almonds

1.2 litres (2 pints) vegetable stock

sea salt and freshly ground black pepper

To serve
crème fraîche or soured cream
freshly chopped flat-leaf parsley
chunky bread

1 > Heat the olive oil in a large saucepan over a medium–high heat. Add the onion, along with a big pinch of salt. Fry for 5 minutes, stirring regularly, until softened. Add the garlic and paprika. Stir and cook for 2 minutes more.

2 > Tip the butternut squash chunks into the pan, along with half of the smoked or roasted almonds. Stir well to combine, then pour in the stock and bring to the boil. Reduce the heat to medium and bubble away for 30 minutes, until the squash is completely softened. Meanwhile, roughly chop the remaining almonds.

3 > Use a stick blender to blend the mixture into a smooth and creamy soup (or blitz, in batches, in a high-speed food processor). Add a little water if it's really thick. Season to taste. It shouldn't need any more salt, as the almonds should salt it enough.

4 > Pour the soup into 4 bowls and top each serving with a dollop of crème fraîche or soured cream. Scatter over the reserved almonds and some freshly chopped parsley and serve with chunky bread.

Tip >
You can roast the squash seeds with a little oil for a great snack.

Photograph overleaf >

SEA BASS, BUTTER BEANS AND SUGAR SNAPS

Cooking fish can sometimes seem a bit scary, especially when you're trying to get perfectly crispy skin. The key is making sure your pan is really hot before you add the fish. Even if it's not perfect, the extra crunch and flavour you get from crisping up the skin is worth giving it a go!

400 g (14 oz) can butter beans

200 ml (7 fl oz) white wine

2 sea bass fillets, skin on, about 85 g (3 oz) each

2 tablespoons olive oil

1 onion, chopped

1 stock cube (vegetable or fish)

3–4 tablespoons store-bought pesto

200 g (7 oz) sugar snap peas (or you can use green beans, or a mixture of both)

100 g (3½ oz) spinach

1 lemon, ½ juiced and ½ cut into wedges

sea salt and freshly ground black pepper

1 > Drain the butter beans through a sieve, but don't rinse them. Pour the white wine into the empty can and set aside.

2 > Place a large non-stick frying pan over a high heat. While the pan is heating up, rub the fish skin with a little olive oil and season well with salt. When the frying pan is hot, place the sea bass in the pan, skin-side down. If the fish curls up, use a spatula or wooden spoon to press it flat. Fry for about 2 minutes until the skin is crisp, then transfer the fillets to a plate. Take the pan off the heat for a minute to cool down a little.

3 > Reduce the heat to medium, return the pan to the heat and add 1 tablespoon olive oil. Add the onion along with a big pinch of salt and cook for about 5 minutes until completely softened. If the onion starts to stick, add a splash of water. Pour in the white wine from the butter beans can. Increase the heat to medium–high, bring to the boil, then bubble until the liquid has reduced by around half.

4 > Refill the can with water, then pour it into the pan along with the stock cube. Stir until the stock cube has dissolved. Tip the butter beans into the mixture and stir. Stir in the pesto and boil for around 5 minutes until the mixture is the consistency of a silky gravy: the starch from the butter beans will thicken up the sauce.

5 > Add the sugar snap peas and cook for around 2 minutes, then add the spinach and the lemon juice and season well. Cook for a further minute or so until the spinach has wilted. Remove from the heat. Carefully place the seabass fillets on top of the mixture, keeping it skin-side up so the skin stays crispy. Leave for a minute or so; the flesh will cook in the heat.

6 > Divide between 2 plates and serve with the lemon wedges.

BEEF PHO

A traditional pho is a wonderful thing. However, attempting it at home can be a lengthy endeavour. This number can be on your table in 15 minutes. Use the best stock you can: a really good liquid stock will take this dish to the next level.

100 g (3½ oz) beef fillet

2 heads of pak choi, separated into leaves

2 handfuls of bean sprouts

handful each of fresh basil and mint leaves

pinch of dried chilli flakes (optional)

1 lime, halved, to serve

For the pho base

thumb-sized piece of fresh root ginger, grated

1 garlic clove, finely sliced

1 small onion, finely sliced

1 tablespoon fish sauce

2 tablespoons soy sauce

3 star anise

100 g (3½ oz) dried flat rice noodles

1 litre (1¾ pints) good-quality beef stock (fresh liquid stock is best if you can get it)

1 teaspoon light brown sugar

1 > If you have time, put your beef in the freezer for 40 minutes before you begin. This will make it much easier to finely slice!

2 > Put all the ingredients for the pho base into a large saucepan and place over a high heat. Boil for 6 minutes.

3 > Meanwhile, finely slice the beef into strips about 3 mm (⅛ in) thick.

4 > Once the pho has been boiling for 6 minutes, add the pak choi and cook for 2 minutes further, until the pak choi and the noodles are cooked through.

5 > Use a pair of tongs to add the noodles and pak choi to the base of 2 bowls. Top with the bean sprouts and sliced beef, then pour the hot broth over the top: this will cook the beef slices. Top with the herbs and a pinch of chilli flakes, if using. Serve each bowl with a lime half for squeezing over.

2
PASTA AND NOODLES

PERFECT PRAWN NOODLES
WITH BROCCOLI AND EDAMAME

This ticks all the boxes for a midweek staple: it's super speedy and you can swap ingredients in and out without compromising on flavour. Swap the prawns for cooked shredded chicken, or scrap them altogether and include extra veggies. Play around with the greens, using sugar snap peas or green beans if you'd prefer. If you don't have tahini, use any nut butter and swap the sesame seeds for any roasted nuts you have to hand.

200 g (7 oz) ready-cooked rice
   noodles (or 100 g/3½ oz dried
   rice noodles, see step 1)
1 tablespoon tahini
1 tablespoon soy sauce
1 tablespoon sriracha
1 lime, ½ juiced and ½ cut into
   wedges
1 tablespoon olive oil
200 g (7 oz) long-stem broccoli,
   cut into 3 cm (1¼ inch) lengths
165 g (5¾ oz) raw king prawns
1 garlic clove, grated
thumb-sized piece of fresh root
   ginger, grated
100 g (3½ oz) frozen edamame
   beans

To serve
sesame seeds
freshly chopped coriander

1 > If using dried rice noodles, place them in a bowl and cover with boiling water. Allow to sit for 10 minutes, then drain and rinse thoroughly. Set aside until needed.

2 > In a small bowl or jug, whisk together the tahini, soy sauce, sriracha and lime juice, along with 2 tablespoons water. Set aside until needed.

3 > Heat the oil in a large non-stick frying pan over a high heat. Add the broccoli to the pan along with 1 tablespoon water and fry for 2–3 minutes, tossing all the time, until the water has evaporated and the broccoli is bright green. Now add the prawns, garlic and ginger and fry everything for 1 minute more. Scatter in the edamame beans and pour over the tahini sauce.

4 > Add the noodles to the pan and toss well to coat in the sauce. Divide between 2 bowls, scatter over the sesame seeds and coriander, and serve with the lime wedges on the side.

FENNEL AND SARDINE ORZO

This is my take on a Sicilian classic. The currants might sound like a strange addition, but their sweetness offsets the saltiness of the anchovies and sardines and makes for the perfect mouthful. If you can't find any orzo, macaroni will work just as well here.

85 g (3 oz) currants or sultanas
175 ml (6 fl oz) white wine
50 g (1¾ oz) can anchovies
2 x 120 g (4¼ oz) cans sardine fillets in olive oil
2 teaspoons fennel seeds
2 fat garlic cloves, finely sliced
2 large fennel bulbs, halved and finely sliced
400 g (14 oz) dried orzo, rinsed
1.2 litres (2 pints) chicken, vegetable or fish stock
juice of 1 lemon
small bunch of fresh dill or parsley, roughly chopped
sea salt and freshly ground black pepper
50 g (1¾ oz) toasted pine nuts, to serve

1 > Place the currants or sultanas in a small bowl. Pour the white wine over them and leave to sit.

2 > Drain the oil from the anchovy and sardine cans into a large saucepan and place the pan over a medium–high heat. Add the anchovies, fennel seeds, garlic and sliced fennel bulbs, along with a pinch of salt. Fry for around 10 minutes, stirring regularly, until everything is soft and slightly browned.

3 > Slosh the wine-and-sultana mixture into the pan and bring to the boil. Add the orzo to the pan and stir to coat, then pour in the stock. Stir well and bring to the boil. Once boiling, reduce the heat a little and cook for 10 minutes, until the orzo is tender, stirring often to keep it from sticking too much.

4 > Reduce the heat to its lowest setting and stir in the lemon juice. Add the sardines, along with most of the chopped dill or parsley, stirring to gently break up the sardines and heat through. Taste and season.

5 > Spoon into 4 bowls. Be sure to scrape off any orzo that has stuck to the base of the pan: that's the best bit. Scatter with the remaining dill or parsley, along with the toasted pine nuts and a crack of black pepper, and serve.

SPINACH LASAGNE... (SORTA)

One of my pals has made this dish almost weekly since I gave her the recipe. It was inspired by the flavours of a spinach and cream cheese pasta from a Jamie Oliver book I loved when I was first learning to cook. Serve with a sharp salad.

1 tablespoon olive oil

2 courgettes, sliced into 5 mm (¼ inch) discs

250 g (9 oz) cream cheese (I use mascarpone)

100 ml (3½ fl oz) double cream

75 g (2½ oz) Parmesan cheese, finely grated

zest of 1 unwaxed lemon (use the juice for a salad dressing)

2 garlic cloves, grated

½ teaspoon ground nutmeg

350 g (12 oz) spinach (or spring greens or kale)

200 g (7 oz) dried lasagne sheets, each one snapped into 3 or 4 pieces

small bunch of fresh basil

sea salt and freshly ground black pepper

toasted pine nuts, to serve

1 > Heat the olive oil in a large non-stick frying pan over a medium–high heat. Add the courgette slices, along with a big pinch of salt, and fry for 8–10 minutes, tossing regularly, until the courgettes are softened and charred in places.

2 > Meanwhile, in a jug, combine the cream cheese, double cream and most of the Parmesan, along with 400 ml (14 fl oz) water. Add the lemon zest, season generously and mix well.

3 > Once the courgettes have softened, add the garlic and nutmeg to the pan and fry for 1 minute. Pour the contents of the jug into the pan and stir until it starts to bubble a little. Now add the spinach and most of the basil: you might have to do this gradually, adding a handful at a time and stirring as it wilts down before adding more.

4 > Once the spinach has completely wilted down, reduce the heat to medium. Add the lasagne pieces. Use your spoon or spatula to make sure they are all submerged and spread out within the sauce.

5 > Cover with a lid and cook for 6 minutes, then give everything a good stir, breaking up any lasagne pieces that might have stuck together. Try to flatten them out: this will create the lasagne feel and make it possible to cut out slices. Scatter with the remaining Parmesan, then cover and cook for 2 minutes further. Check that it's cooked through: a knife should slide through without any resistance. If not, cover with a lid and cook for 2 minutes further.

6 > Remove from the heat and leave to sit for 5 minutes, then scatter over the remaining basil leaves and pine nuts. Use a spatula to divide into 4 portions and serve straight out of the pan at the table.

Photograph overleaf >

HOT-SMOKED SALMON AND CRÈME FRAÎCHE PASTA

I feel like I ate a version of this growing up – probably one from a Mary Berry cookbook – so it's got a hit of nostalgia to it. It also manages to be both fresh and indulgent in equal measure, plus it's ready in 30 minutes. The perfect midweek dinner to feed the whole household.

2 tablespoons olive oil

2 celery sticks, finely sliced

1 garlic clove, grated

2 stock cubes (fish or vegetable)

400 g (14 oz) dried spaghetti

200 ml (7 fl oz) crème fraîche

200 g (7 oz) frozen peas

small bunch of fresh flat-leaf parsley or dill, roughly chopped

180 g (6½ oz) hot-smoked salmon, broken up into chunks

1 lemon, ½ juiced and ½ cut into wedges

sea salt and freshly ground black pepper

1 > Heat the olive oil in a deep saucepan over a medium–high heat. Add the celery, along with a big pinch of salt, and fry for around 5 minutes, until softened. Add the garlic and fry for 2 more minutes. Pour 1.2 litres (2 pints) water into the pan, along with the stock cubes. Bring to the boil and stir to make sure the stock cubes have dissolved.

2 > Add the spaghetti, cover with a lid and cook for 8–10 minutes, until the spaghetti is nearly cooked and the stock/water has reduced.

3 > Stir in the crème fraîche and frozen peas, along with most of the parsley or dill. Cook for 2 minutes, until the peas have defrosted and are bright green. Remove from the heat. Gently stir the smoked salmon chunks into the pasta. Add the lemon juice and season well.

4 > Swirl into 4 bowls, and top with the remaining parsley or dill and a crack of black pepper. Serve with the lemon wedges, for squeezing over at the table.

SAUSAGE AND BROCCOLI GNOCCHI

If you want to make a veggie/vegan version of this dish, you can use veggie mince, or skip this element altogether. However, the crispy chunks of sausage meat make it all the more tasty to me! If you have a food processor or mini chopper, it will come in handy for this recipe, but it's not essential.

2 tablespoons olive oil

4 sausages, or around 200 g (7 oz) pork mince

1 teaspoon fennel seeds

½ head of broccoli, broken into florets

small bunch of fresh flat-leaf parsley

300 g (10½ oz) gnocchi

1 garlic clove, grated

juice of 1 lemon

sea salt and freshly ground black pepper

To serve

grated Parmesan cheese

toasted pine nuts

1 > Heat 1 tablespoon olive oil in a large non-stick frying pan over a medium–high heat. Squeeze the meat out of the sausages directly into the pan, or if using pork mince, add it to the pan. Fry for 6–8 minutes, then add the fennel seeds and fry for 2 minutes further, until the meat is browned.

2 > Meanwhile, add the broccoli and most of the parsley to the food processor and pulse a couple of times. You want the broccoli to be roughly chopped, but not blitzed. If you don't have a food processor, chop the broccoli florets into chunky crumbs, chop most of the parsley and mix together.

3 > Once the meat has browned, add the gnocchi and 75 ml (2½ fl oz) water to the pan. Cook for 2–3 minutes until the water has evaporated. Add the remaining olive oil to the pan and toss everything together well. Fry for a couple of minutes; you want the gnocchi to get a little crispy. Add the garlic and fry for 1 minute more.

4 > Tip the broccoli and parsley mixture into the pan and toss again. Stir through the lemon juice and season with salt and pepper. Cook for 5 minutes until the broccoli is cooked through.

5 > Serve in bowls, topped with a generous grating of Parmesan, a scattering of pine nuts and the remaining parsley.

ALL-IN-ONE SPAGHETTI AND MEATBALLS

This is the perfect date-night dinner. It's easy but impressive, and the big reveal of the glossy tomato sauce coating perfectly cooked spaghetti and meatballs is sure to get anyone swooning.

250 g (9 oz) beef mince
1 small onion, finely chopped
1 teaspoon dried oregano
1 egg
1 tablespoon olive oil
1 garlic clove, grated
1 tablespoon tomato puree
100 ml (3½ fl oz) red wine
500 ml (18 fl oz) passata (sieved tomatoes)
1 stock cube (vegetable or chicken)
200 g (7 oz) dried spaghetti
salt and freshly ground black pepper

To serve
fresh basil
grated Parmesan cheese

1 > In a large bowl, mix together the beef mince with the onion, dried oregano, egg and a big pinch of salt and pepper. Roll into 10 balls.

2 > Heat the olive oil in a large non-stick frying pan over a high heat. Once hot, add the meatballs and fry for around 3 minutes until golden. Shake the pan so they roll around and get an even colour. Reduce the heat to medium.

3 > Add the garlic and tomato puree and stir into the juices in the pan until the garlic is colouring slightly. Add the red wine and bubble for 2 minutes, until it is reduced by half, then add the passata.

4 > Pour 300 ml (10 fl oz) water into the pan and crumble in the stock cube. Bring to the boil, season with salt and pepper, then add the spaghetti. Make sure the spaghetti is submerged: you can break it a little if you need to. Reduce the heat slightly, cover with a lid, then simmer for 10 minutes, stirring every now and then to stop the pasta sticking to the base of the pan. If the spaghetti doesn't seem quite cooked, just add a splash more water and continue to cook until the spaghetti is done to your liking.

5 > Once the spaghetti is cooked and you are left with a juicy, thick tomato sauce coating everything, remove the pan from the heat. Top with fresh basil and grated Parmesan and serve.

THAI GREEN SEA BASS AND RICE NOODLES

This is one for when you're a little short of time. It's light and fresh, while also managing to be incredibly satisfying.

200 g (7 oz) ready-cooked rice noodles (or 100 g/3½ oz dried rice noodles, see step 1)

2 sea bass fillets, skin on, about 90 g (3¼ oz) each

2–3 tablespoons Thai green curry paste (depending on the strength of the paste)

1–2 tablespoons sesame, vegetable or olive oil (I like to use sesame oil for this recipe)

200 g (7 oz) long-stem broccoli, roughly chopped

4 spring onions, finely sliced

pinch of dried chilli flakes (optional)

1 garlic clove, grated

thumb-sized piece of fresh root ginger, grated

1 tablespoon soy sauce

1 lime, ½ juiced and ½ cut into wedges

To serve

basil leaves (Thai basil if you can find it)

toasted sesame seeds

1 > If using dried rice noodles, place them in a bowl and cover with boiling water. Allow to sit for 10 minutes, then drain and rinse thoroughly. Set aside until needed.

2 > Coat the sea bass with the Thai green curry paste and a little of the oil. Place a large non-stick frying pan over a high heat. You want the frying pan to be hot before you add the fish, so that the fish skin will get nice and crispy without cooking the whole fish. When the frying pan is hot, place the sea bass in the pan, skin-side down. If the fish curls up, use your spatula or wooden spoon to press it flat. Fry for about 2 minutes until the skin is crisp, then transfer the fillets to a plate. Take the pan off the heat for a minute to cool down a little.

3 > Heat 1 tablespoon oil in the frying pan over a medium–high heat. Add the broccoli and toss for 2 minutes. Add the spring onions and chilli flakes, if using. Add the garlic and ginger, toss well and cook for 1 minute further. Add the soy sauce and lime juice, then add the rice noodles to the pan along with a big splash of water. Toss well to coat.

4 > Place the sea bass fillets on top, skin-side up so the skin stays crispy, and cook for 2 minutes, until the fish flesh is cooked through. Scatter over the basil and toasted sesame seeds and serve with the lime wedges.

TURMERIC AND GINGER CHICKEN NOODLES

This is one of my all-time favourite recipes. It's indulgent, but it also feels balanced and kind of fresh. Also, ever slurp-able udon noodles are never not a great addition to a meal in my eyes.

1 tablespoon olive, sesame or coconut oil

bunch of spring onions, finely sliced

1 garlic clove, grated

3 cm (1¼ inch) chunk of fresh root ginger, grated

2 teaspoons ground turmeric

pinch of dried chilli flakes, plus extra to serve (optional)

400 ml (14 fl oz) can coconut milk

1 chicken stock cube

6 skinless, boneless chicken thighs, about 500 g (1 lb 2oz) in total

2 limes, 1 juiced and 1 cut into wedges

1 tablespoon soy sauce

1 teaspoon clear honey or sugar

400 g (14 oz) ready-cooked udon noodles (or use other ready-cooked noodles of your choice)

sea salt and freshly ground black pepper

To serve

a few handfuls of roasted peanuts, roughly chopped

freshly chopped coriander

1 > Heat the oil in a large non-stick frying pan over a medium–high heat. Add the spring onions with a big pinch of salt and cook for around 2 minutes. Add the garlic and ginger and fry for 1 minute further, then add the turmeric and chilli flakes (if using) and stir to combine. Fry for 1 minute, then pour in the coconut milk. Half-fill the emptied can with water and pour that into the pan too, along with the stock cube. Bring to the boil and stir to ensure the stock cube has dissolved.

2 > Reduce the heat to low and nestle the chicken thighs into the pan. Cover and leave to bubble very gently for 12–15 minutes. Make sure it's gentle or the chicken will be tough! If your chicken thighs are large, they might take a little longer to cook through.

3 > Once the chicken is cooked through, use two forks to shred it in the pan. If you find it easier, you can lift the chicken pieces out of the pan and shred them on a plate or board, then return to the pan. Increase the heat to medium–high. Add the lime juice, along with the soy sauce and honey or sugar, then tip in the noodles. Stir to combine. Taste and season well.

4 > Divide between 4 bowls and scatter with the peanuts and coriander, as well as some more chilli flakes if you like a bit of spice! Serve with the lime wedges.

Photograph overleaf >

SPICY AND CRISPY SICHUAN 'NOODLES'

*This cheat's version of hand-pulled noodles is just as good as the real thing.
The crispy chilli oil is what you're really here for. You can use mince instead
of mushrooms if you would like a meaty version.*

small splash of vegetable or
sunflower oil

500 g (1 lb 2 oz) mixed
mushrooms, large ones roughly
chopped and small ones kept
whole

1 small bunch spring onions,
finely sliced

1 tablespoon tahini (optional)

3 tablespoons soy sauce, plus
extra to serve

2 limes, 1 juiced and 1 cut into
wedges

350 g (12 oz) fresh egg tagliatelle

sea salt and freshly ground black
pepper

For the crispy chilli oil

50 ml (2 fl oz) sunflower or
vegetable oil

1 red chilli, finely sliced

1 garlic clove, finely sliced

thumb-sized piece of fresh
root ginger, sliced into thin
matchsticks

½ teaspoon Sichuan
peppercorns, roughly chopped
or crushed (if you can't find
these, use 1 teaspoon five
spice powder

1 tablespoon sesame seeds

1 teaspoon hot chilli powder

1 > To make the crispy chilli oil, pour the oil into a large non-stick frying
pan, off the heat. Add the remaining ingredients, then place the pan
over a medium heat. Cook for around 10 minutes. Keep shaking the
pan and keep a close eye on it: you want to remove it from the heat
as soon as the garlic starts to turn slightly golden.

2 > Pour the hot oil into a bowl, using a spatula to make sure you get it all
out. Set aside.

3 > Place the pan over a high heat and add a small splash of oil. Add the
mushrooms to the pan, along with a big pinch of salt, and fry for
10–15 minutes, tossing regularly, until they are completely softened
and charred in places.

4 > Meanwhile, in a small jug, mix together the tahini (if using), soy sauce
and lime juice, along with 300 ml (10 fl oz) water. Season well and set
aside until needed.

5 > When the mushrooms are soft and charred, add most of the spring
onion slices and cook for 2–3 minutes further. Reduce the heat a little
and pour the liquid from the jug into the pan, along with the tagliatelle.
Cook for 5–6 minutes, tossing repeatedly, using the tongs to break
up the tagliatelle, until the pasta is cooked through and coated in the
sauce. Add more water if it starts to go claggy at all.

6 > Spoon into 4 bowls, then drizzle the crispy chilli oil over the top, mixing
it in as you eat. Serve with the lime wedges and extra soy sauce.

DOLLED-UP TORTELLINI

This is how to use a store-bought item (tortellini) and elevate it to create an elegant and impressive dinner. I love serving this with a fennel salad, with the fennel sliced as thinly as possible and tossed with loads of lemon juice.

1 tablespoon olive oil
2 garlic cloves, grated
1 stock cube (vegetable or chicken)
600 g (1 lb 5 oz) tortellini (I use spinach and ricotta)
200 g (7 oz) frozen peas
large bunch of fresh herbs, roughly chopped (I use flat-leaf parsley or dill)
juice of 1 lemon
50 g (1¾ oz) Parmesan cheese, finely grated
sea salt and freshly ground black pepper

1 > Heat the olive oil in a large frying pan over a medium heat. Add the garlic and cook for 1 minute, then add 300 ml (10 fl oz) water and the stock cube. Bring to the boil, stirring to make sure the stock cube has dissolved.

2 > Add the tortellini to the pan. Cover with a lid and cook for 3–4 minutes, shaking the pan regularly so the tortellini doesn't stick to the base. Remove the lid and add the peas. Stir in most of the herbs and half the lemon juice. Season well with salt and pepper and toss to combine. Cook for 2 minutes, until the peas are bright green. Now add most of the Parmesan to the pan and keep tossing as it melts into the starchy water to create a silky sauce. Taste and add more lemon juice if you feel it needs it.

3 > Split between 4 bowls, top with the remaining herbs and Parmesan, and serve.

PASTA E FAGIOLI

Traditionally, this is made with handmade pasta and beans that have been soaked, then slowly braised. This version uses some short cuts to speed up the process, but it still feels rustic. I love serving this with a fat spoonful of ricotta and some warm chunky bread.

1.5 litres (2¾ pints) hot vegetable stock
a pinch of saffron (optional)
1 tablespoon olive oil, plus extra for drizzling
1 onion, finely chopped
2 carrots, not peeled, halved lengthways and sliced into 3 mm (⅛ inch) half-moon pieces
2 celery sticks, sliced into 3 mm (⅛ inch) slices
2 cloves garlic, finely sliced
4 sun-dried tomatoes, roughly chopped
1 tablespoon tomato puree
400 g (14 oz) can borlotti beans
125 g (4½ oz) small pasta shapes (I use farfelle)
juice of 1 lemon or 1 tablespoon red wine vinegar
small bunch of fresh basil or flat-leaf parsley, roughly chopped
sea salt and freshly ground black pepper

1 > If using saffron, add it to the vegetable stock, stir and set aside.

2 > Heat the olive oil in a large saucepan over a medium heat. Add the onion, carrots and celery, along with a pinch of salt, and fry for around 10 minutes, stirring regularly, until softened.

3 > Add the garlic and sundried tomatoes to the pan and fry for 2 minutes, then stir in the tomato puree and fry for 1 minute further. Tip in the whole can of borlotti beans, including the liquid from the can. Add the stock, then increase the heat to high and bring to the boil.

4 > Add the pasta to the pan, reduce the heat back to medium, cover the pan with a lid and cook for 10–12 minutes, until the pasta is cooked through. Add the lemon juice or vinegar, along with most of the fresh herbs. Season with a little salt and pepper.

5 > Allow to rest for 2–3 minutes off the heat, then spoon the soup into 4 bowls. Top each one with a drizzle of olive oil and a scattering of the remaining basil or parsley leaves, and serve.

TRIPLE TOMATO RIGATONI

Sundried, fresh and tinned – three kinds of tomato combine here to make one dream sauce. Make it veggie by using vegetable stock and replacing the chorizo with 2 teaspoons smoked paprika.

1 tablespoon olive oil

2 chubby garlic cloves, grated or crushed

1 tablespoon dried oregano (optional)

2 x 400 g (14 oz) can chopped tomatoes

1 stock cube (vegetable or chicken)

300 g (10½ oz) cherry tomatoes

400 g (14 oz) rigatoni or any chunky small pasta shapes

75 g (2½ oz) sun-dried tomatoes, roughly chopped

1 tablespoon balsamic vinegar

sea salt and freshly ground black pepper

To serve
feta cheese
basil leaves

1 > Heat the olive oil in a large saucepan over a medium heat. Add the garlic to the pan and fry for 2 minutes. Sprinkle in the dried oregano, if using, along with a big pinch of salt. Stir, then tip in the chopped tomatoes. Refill one of the emptied cans with water and pour that into the pan too. Increase the heat to high. Crumble in the stock cube and half the fresh cherry tomatoes, stir well to combine, then bring to the boil.

2 > Stir in the pasta. Reduce the heat to medium, cover with a lid and cook for the length of time indicated on the pasta packet (usually around 10–12 minutes), stirring regularly so the pasta doesn't stick to the base of the pan. (If the pasta does stick, add a splash more water.)

3 > Meanwhile, cut the remaining cherry tomatoes in half.

4 > When the pasta is cooked, stir through the cherry tomato halves, along with the sun-dried tomatoes and the balsamic vinegar. Season well and spoon into bowls. Serve topped with crumbled feta and fresh basil leaves.

3
RISOTTOS, GRAINS AND PULSES GALORE

LEEK AND BLACK PEPPER RISOTTO

All the flavours of cacio e pepe, a traditional Italian cheese and pepper pasta dish, but with the added advantage of soft, sweet leeks. I love serving this with a wedge of garlic bread and a punchy green salad. Omit the anchovies for a vegetarian option.

1 teaspoon black peppercorns

2 tablespoons unsalted butter

3 large leeks, trimmed, cleaned and finely sliced

bunch of spring onions, finely sliced

2 garlic cloves, finely sliced

2 teaspoons fennel seeds

300 g (10½ oz) risotto rice

200 ml (7 fl oz) white wine

1.3 litres (2½ pints) vegetable or chicken stock

75 g (2½ oz) Parmesan cheese, grated

1 unwaxed lemon

sea salt

50 g (1¾ oz) toasted pine nuts, to serve

1 > Tip the peppercorns into a large saucepan over a medium–high heat. Toast the peppercorns for 2 minutes, then tip on to a chopping board. Use the side of a knife to crush the peppercorns, then finely chop. Set aside in a small bowl.

2 > Melt 1 tablespoon butter in the saucepan over a medium heat. Add the leeks and spring onions with a big pinch of salt. Fry for around 10 minutes, stirring regularly, until soft but not coloured. If they start to catch on the base, add a splash of water and reduce the heat a little.

3 > Add the garlic and fennel seeds to the pan and fry for 2 more minutes. Add the risotto rice and stir to coat. Toast for 1 minute, then add the wine and cook until the liquid is reduced by half. Add a big glug of the stock and cook until absorbed, stirring occasionally. Continue to add the stock, adding a little more as each addition is absorbed.

4 > Once all the stock has been added, and the rice is cooked through, the mixture should be a soupy consistency. Stir in the grated Parmesan and most of the black pepper, as well as the remaining butter.

5 > Spoon the risotto into 4 bowls and top with the pine nuts and the remaining black pepper. Zest over the lemon, then cut into wedges to serve on the side.

LEMON AND OREGANO CHICKEN AND RICE

Using both fresh and preserved lemons, this is a double-whammy lemon dish.
It's not just delicious, it's also easy-peasy...(lemon squeezy).

2 tablespoons olive oil

8 skinless, boneless chicken thighs, about 650 g (1 lb 7 oz) in total

1 preserved lemon, flesh and pips removed and discarded, and skin finely chopped

2 garlic cloves, finely sliced

1 green chilli, finely sliced

1 tablespoon dried oregano (or half a bunch of fresh oregano leaves, if you can find some!)

150 ml (5 fl oz) white wine

250 g (9 oz) basmati rice, rinsed well and drained

850 ml (1½ pints) chicken or vegetable stock

2 medium-sized courgettes, coarsely grated

100 g (3½ oz) green olives, halved

bunch of fresh flat-leaf parsley or fresh dill, roughly chopped

1 lemon, cut into wedges

sea salt and freshly ground black pepper

1 > Heat 1 tablespoon of the olive oil in your largest non-stick, high-sided frying pan over a high heat. Season the chicken thighs, then add them to the pan and fry for 2–3 minutes on each side, until golden. Transfer the chicken thighs to a plate and set aside.

2 > Reduce the heat to medium and add the remaining olive oil. Add the preserved lemon, garlic, green chilli and oregano, along with a big pinch of salt. Fry for about 2 minutes, until everything is softening and beginning to colour.

3 > Pour the white wine into the pan. Add the rice, stir well, then pour in the stock and bring back to the boil. Once boiling, reduce the heat to a simmer, snuggle the chicken thighs into the rice and cover the pan with a lid. Leave to simmer for 10 minutes.

4 > Fold the courgettes, olives and most of the chopped herbs through the rice mixture. Pour in a splash of water, put the lid back on the pan and cook for 5 minutes more until the rice and chicken are cooked through.

5 > Scatter with the remaining herbs and serve with the lemon wedges.

CAJUN PRAWN RICE
WITH MANGO AND CHILLI SALSA

Spicy, fresh and on the table in 20 minutes. This is the speediest way to get that holiday feeling, all in one bowl.

125 g (4½ oz) mango, cut into ½ cm (¼ inch) cubes (see Tip)

1 red chilli, finely chopped (deseeded if you don't want it to be spicy!)

bunch of spring onions, finely sliced

small bunch of fresh mint, roughly chopped

juice of 1 lime or lemon

2 tablespoons olive oil

1 garlic clove, grated

thumb-sized piece of fresh root ginger, grated

2 teaspoons Cajun seasoning

165 g (5¾ oz) raw prawns

250 g (9 oz) pouch ready-cooked basmati rice

sea salt and freshly ground black pepper

1 > Begin by making the mango and chilli salsa. In a small bowl, combine the mango with half the red chilli, half the spring onions and half the mint. Squeeze in half the lime/lemon juice and add 1 tablespoon olive oil. Season well with salt and pepper and toss everything together. Set aside until needed.

2 > Heat the remaining olive oil in a large non-stick, high-sided frying pan over a medium–high heat. Add the remaining red chilli and spring onions. Stir in the garlic, ginger and Cajun seasoning. Fry for 2 minutes, then add the prawns and cook for 2 minutes, tossing, until the prawns have turned pink and are golden in places.

3 > Tip the rice into the pan, add a splash of water, and toss for 2 more minutes. Stir in the remaining mint and lime/lemon juice and season well. Divide between 2 bowls and serve with the salsa.

Tip >
If you're using a whole mango, cut off the sides so you have two 'cheeks'. (You can peel and snack on the flesh around the core). Use a sharp knife to slice a cross-hatch pattern into each of the mango 'cheeks', then turn them inside out so the cubes pop up. Slide a knife under the cubes and pop them out on to a chopping board.

CRISPY LAMB RICE
WITH MINT ZHOUG

My brother made a version of this by accident when using up items from our fridge. I refined it a bit and the minty zhoug lifts everything. If you don't have a mini chopper, you can crush the spices in a pestle and mortar and finely chop the herbs with a knife.

1 tablespoon ground coriander

1 tablespoon cumin seeds

2 aubergines, cut into 3 cm (1¼ inch) chunks

500 g (1 lb 2 oz) lamb mince

2½–3½ tablespoons olive oil

1 red onion, finely chopped

1 garlic clove, peeled

½ teaspoon chilli powder

1 tablespoon za'atar (optional)

2 x 250 g (9 oz) pouches of ready-cooked rice

juice of 2 lemons

small bunch of fresh mint, roughly chopped

small bunch of fresh flat-leaf parsley, roughly chopped

sea salt and freshly ground black pepper

To serve

pomegranate seeds

hummus (optional)

1 > Heat a large non-stick frying pan over a high heat. Add the ground coriander and cumin seeds and toast for a couple of minutes, then tip the toasted spices into a mini chopper and blitz. Set aside.

2 > Wipe out the pan, then add the aubergine chunks and dry-fry for around 5 minutes, until they are beginning to char.

3 > Add the lamb to the frying pan, along with half a tablespoon olive oil. Fry for 10–12 minutes, until the lamb is crisp and the aubergine chunks have collapsed. The aubergine chunks will soak up some of the oil from the lamb.

4 > Add the red onion and fry for a couple more minutes, then grate the garlic into the pan. Add half the spices from the mini chopper, along with the chilli powder and za'atar, if using. Stir-fry for another minute, then tip the rice into the pan, along with a splash of water. Use a spoon to break up the rice and stir well for 2 minutes. Remove from the heat, squeeze over the juice of 1 lemon, and season well.

5 > Scatter over a small handful each of the fresh mint and parsley and toss through the rice.

6 > Put the remaining mint and parsley in the mini chopper with the rest of the ground coriander and blitzed cumin seeds. Add the juice of the remaining lemon and 2–3 tablespoons olive oil. Season well with salt and pepper and blitz to create a green zhoug sauce.

7 > Drizzle the mint zhoug on top of the rice and scatter with pomegranate seeds, then serve. If you like, add a dollop of hummus.

RED CABBAGE AND SAUSAGE FRIED RICE

The age-old combo of sausage and red cabbage gets a punchy makeover in this fried rice. Don't worry if you can't get your hands on any miso, this is delicious without it. However, if you can find some, then use it – it will take this dish to the next level!

¼ head of red cabbage, finely sliced

2 limes, 1 juiced and 1 cut into wedges

1 teaspoon sesame oil

3 chunky pork sausages

thumb-sized piece of fresh root ginger, grated

1 garlic clove, grated

½ red chilli, seeds removed if you don't like spice, finely chopped

1 tablespoon miso paste (optional)

250 g (9 oz) pouch ready-cooked rice

2 tablespoons soy sauce

sea salt and freshly ground black pepper

To serve
sesame seeds
freshly chopped coriander

1 > Put the sliced red cabbage in a large bowl and pour over the lime juice. Add a big pinch of salt and squeeze the cabbage with your hands. Set aside until needed. This will lightly pickle the cabbage, giving it loads of flavour.

2 > Heat the sesame oil in a large high-sided frying pan over a high heat. Squeeze the meat out of the sausages into the pan, and stir-fry until the sausage meat is starting to caramelize and crisp up. Be patient: this can take 10–12 minutes. Scoop out a spoonful of the crispy sausage and set aside.

3 > Add the ginger, garlic and chilli to the pan. Cook for a couple of minutes, then add the miso, if using, and stir well. Tip the red cabbage into the pan, along with any lime juice from the bowl. Fry for 2 minutes, then add the rice, along with a big splash of water. Add the soy sauce and toss well. Cook for 2 minutes until everything is heated through, then season.

4 > Top with the reserved crispy sausage, sesame seeds and chopped coriander, and serve with the lime wedges on the side.

Photograph overleaf >

BLACK DHAL (ISH)

This is a cheat. It's not the slowly cooked black dhal of our favourite Indian restaurants, but it still hits the spot: it's rich and hearty, without being too heavy. A mini chopper will come in really handy for this recipe.

400 g (14 oz) can black beans

1 tablespoon tomato puree

1 red onion, finely chopped

2 limes

1 tablespoon coconut, vegetable or olive oil

1 red chilli, finely chopped

thumb-sized piece of fresh root ginger, grated

1 garlic clove, grated

1 teaspoon ground cumin

1 teaspoon ground coriander

250 g (9 oz) cherry tomatoes, three-quarters left whole and the rest roughly chopped

400 ml (14 fl oz) can coconut milk

2 x 250 g (9 oz) pouches ready-cooked puy lentils

small bunch of fresh coriander, roughly chopped

sea salt and freshly ground black pepper

coconut yogurt, to serve

1 > Place half the beans from the can in the mini chopper, along with the tomato puree. Blitz to form a paste. If you don't have a mini chopper, simply mash half the beans in a bowl with the tomato puree until you have a paste-like consistency. Set aside until needed.

2 > Place 1 tablespoon of the chopped red onion in a bowl. Season with some salt and squeeze the juice of 1 lime over the top. Mix it together with your hands and set aside until needed.

3 > Heat the oil in a large saucepan over a medium–high heat. Add the remaining onion to the pan, along with the chilli and a big pinch of salt. Fry for a couple of minutes, until the onion softens, then add the ginger, garlic, ground cumin and ground coriander. Stir and cook for a couple of minutes, to make sure the dhal doesn't taste of raw spice.

4 > Add the black bean and tomato puree mixture to the pan and stir, then add the whole cherry tomatoes. Fry for 3 minutes, until the tomato skins start to split, then pour in the coconut milk. Empty the pouches of lentils into the pan, along with the remaining half can of black beans, plus any liquid in the can. Add a big splash of water, season well with salt and stir to combine thoroughly. Reduce the heat to medium and cook for 10 minutes, until everything is thick and rich.

5 > While the dhal is bubbling away, make the cherry tomato topping. Add the chopped cherry tomatoes and fresh coriander to the bowl containing the red onion and lime juice mixture. Season well and toss.

6 > Add the juice of half the remaining lime to the dhal. Slice the remaining lime half into wedges. Spoon the dhal into 4 bowls, swirl a spoonful of coconut yogurt over each one, and top with some of the cherry tomato topping. Serve with the lime wedges for squeezing over.

BLOODY MARY RISOTTO

People don't tend to use tomatoes in a risotto, or vodka for that matter, but this dish is one of the tastiest risottos I've ever made. It's a great vegan option if you leave out the feta. It's best eaten in the middle of summer, when tomatoes are at their absolute best!

1 tablespoon olive oil, plus extra to serve

3 celery sticks, finely sliced

1 red onion, chopped

2 garlic cloves, finely sliced

1 tablespoon tomato puree

300 g (10½ oz) risotto rice

75 ml (2½ fl oz) vodka

400 g (14 oz) cherry tomatoes

1.7 litres (3 pints) vegetable stock

3 tablespoons capers

1 lemon

sea salt and freshly ground black pepper

To serve

Tabasco and/or Worcestershire sauce (optional)

feta cheese, crumbled

fresh basil leaves

1 > Heat the oil in a large saucepan over a medium–high heat. Add the celery and red onion, along with a big pinch of salt, and fry for 10 minutes until softened.

2 > Add the garlic and cook for 1 minute, then add the tomato puree and stir so it coats all of the veg. Tip the risotto rice into the pan and stir well. Toast the rice for about 1 minute, then add 50 ml (2 fl oz) of the vodka, along with the cherry tomatoes.

3 > Reduce the heat a little and add a big splash of stock. Once it has been absorbed into the rice, add a little more. Continue to do this, adding the stock a splash at a time, for 20–25 minutes, until the rice is nearly cooked, but with a little bite, and the risotto has a thick, soupy consistency. You might not need all the stock.

4 > Stir in the capers and squeeze over the juice of ½ lemon. Season well and remove from the heat. Add a splash of Tabasco and/or Worcestershire sauce, if using, then add the remaining vodka. Spoon the risotto into bowls and top with some crumbled feta, basil and a drizzle of olive oil. Finish with a crack of black pepper and serve with the remaining ½ lemon, cut into wedges.

ALL-THE-GREENS RISOTTO

There's so much green in this that it could be mistaken for a health juice, but don't worry – it's not! It is, in fact, the most banging risotto you've ever tasted. Serve it with a big green salad, to stick with the green theme. You'll need a mini chopper or food processor for this recipe.

1 tablespoon olive oil
2 celery sticks, finely chopped
1 garlic clove, finely sliced
300 g (10½ oz) risotto rice
200 ml (7 fl oz) white wine
1.5 litres (2¾ pints) vegetable
   stock
200 g (7 oz) spinach
large bunch of fresh herbs
   (I use a mixture of parsley,
   coriander and dill)
juice of 1 lemon
1 tablespoon salted butter
25 g (1 oz) Parmesan cheese,
   finely grated
sea salt and freshly ground black
   pepper

1 > Heat the olive oil in a large non-stick, high-sided frying pan over a medium heat. Add the celery, along with a big pinch of salt, and gently fry for 6–8 minutes, until soft but not coloured. Add the garlic and cook for 2 minutes further.

2 > Tip the rice into the pan and stir to coat in the oil. Toast for 1 minute, then pour in the wine. Bubble for a couple of minutes, until the liquid is reduced by half. Reduce the heat a little and add a big splash of stock. Once it's absorbed into the rice, add a little more. Continue to do this for around 20 minutes, until the rice is nearly cooked, but with a little bite, and the risotto has a thick, soupy consistency – you might not need to use all of the stock.

3 > Meanwhile, place the spinach, most of the herbs and the lemon juice into a food processor or mini chopper, along with a big splash of the stock. Blitz to form a puree and season well.

4 > Once the risotto has been cooking for 20 minutes, add the puree and stir well: it will turn your risotto bright green. Add the butter and most of the Parmesan, taste and season. Add another splash of stock or water to loosen the risotto if needed.

5 > Serve the risotto in bowls, topped with the remaining Parmesan and herbs and a crack of black pepper.

BRASSICA BOWL

WITH TAHINI YOGURT

I can honestly say that I eat a version of this once a week. It's really easy to vary the veg, change up the grains or scatter with different toasted seeds and nuts. You can also easily add extra spices, trying out different combos and making it your own. It's healthy and fresh, plus it's veggie – or easily vegan, if you swap in coconut yogurt. Basically, it's a winner-winner midweek dinner.

1 tablespoon olive oil

small bunch of spring onions, sliced into 3 cm (1¼ inch) lengths

250 g (9 oz) long-stem broccoli, sliced into 3 cm (1¼ inch) lengths, or 1 whole head of broccoli, cut into florets

2 tablespoons tahini

100 ml (3½ fl oz) natural yogurt

juice of 1 lemon

1 garlic clove, grated

1 teaspoon ground coriander

1 teaspoon fennel seeds

2 x 250 g (9 oz) pouches mixed grains (or a mixture of cooked rice and puy lentils)

handful of fresh herbs, roughly chopped (I use parsley and coriander)

sea salt and freshly ground black pepper

To serve

dried chilli flakes

roasted almonds, chopped

1 > Heat the olive oil in a large non-stick frying pan over a high heat. Add the spring onions and broccoli, along with a big pinch of salt. Fry for 5 minutes, tossing regularly, until softened and charred in places.

2 > Meanwhile, in a small bowl, mix together the tahini and yogurt. Season and add half the lemon juice. It should be a drizzle-able consistency: add a little water if it thickens too much. Set aside until needed.

3 > Once the spring onions and broccoli have been cooking for 5 minutes, add the garlic, ground coriander and fennel seeds and toss everything well to combine. Squeeze the pouches of grains a little in your hands to loosen up the contents, then tip them into the pan and toss well. Add a splash of water and cook for a minute, until the grains are heated through. Stir in the remaining lemon juice and most of the fresh herbs. Taste and season with salt and pepper.

4 > To serve, drizzle over the tahini yogurt and scatter with the remaining chopped herbs. Top with a pinch of dried chilli flakes and chopped roasted almonds.

Photograph overleaf >

CHIPOTLE BLACK BEANS
WITH AVOCADO, SOURED CREAM AND CHILLI FLAKES

I love beans and these are no exception to the rule. This dish has the vibe of a really good burrito, but it's also warm and homey in the way only a bowl of soupy beans can be. To make this dish vegan, just leave out the soured cream.

1 tablespoon olive oil
1 red onion, sliced
1 garlic clove, grated
1 tablespoon chipotle paste
1 tablespoon tomato puree
2 x 400 g (14 oz) cans black beans
1 vegetable stock cube
2 large tomatoes, roughly
    chopped
340 g (12 oz) can sweetcorn
juice of 1 lime
small bunch of freshly chopped
    coriander
sea salt and freshly ground black
    pepper

To serve
2 avocados, peeled, stoned
    and sliced
soured cream
dried chilli flakes
tortilla chips

1 > Heat the olive oil in a large saucepan over a medium heat. Add the onion and fry for 6–8 minutes, until softened.

2 > Add the garlic, stir, and cook for 2 minutes, then add the chipotle paste and tomato puree, and fry for 2 minutes more. Add the beans, along with the liquid from their cans, and crumble in the stock cube. Add the chopped tomatoes and a splash of water and bring to the boil, then reduce to a simmer and cook for 15 minutes. Season well.

3 > Add the sweetcorn, along with the water from the can. Stir in the lime juice and most of the coriander, then check the seasoning, adding a little more lime juice or salt to taste.

4 > Divide the beans between 4 bowls. Top each one with some sliced avocado and a dollop of soured cream, and scatter with the remaining coriander. Add a pinch of dried chilli flakes, if you like. Serve with tortilla chips for scooping up.

KITCHARI

This is a famous Ayurvedic dish. It's so soothing, it feels a bit like you're hugging your soul when you eat it. My top tip would be to make it on a Sunday and make enough to eat it again a day later when the flavours have developed and that Monday feeling has kicked in.

2 tablespoons coconut, sunflower or olive oil

2 courgettes, chopped into 2 cm (¾ inch) chunks

thumb-sized piece of fresh root ginger, grated

1 teaspoon mustard seeds

1 teaspoon fennel seeds

1 teaspoon ground coriander

2 teaspoons ground turmeric

150 g (5¼ oz) brown rice

150 g (5¼ oz) split yellow peas (or use red or green lentils)

1.2 litres (2 pints) vegetable stock

300 g (10½ oz) spinach

150 ml (5 fl oz) coconut yogurt

1 lemon or lime, ½ juiced and ½ cut into wedges

sea salt and freshly ground black pepper

freshly chopped coriander, to serve

1 > Heat the oil in a large saucepan over a high heat. Add the courgettes, along with a big pinch of salt, and fry for around 8 minutes until lightly charred and collapsing. Add the ginger, followed by the spices, and stir so that everything is well coated. Fry for 1 minute until fragrant. Add the brown rice and split yellow peas to the pan and stir again.

2 > Pour in the vegetable stock. Bring to the boil, then reduce the heat to a simmer. Season, then cover with a lid and cook for 40–45 minutes, stirring regularly. At this point, the rice and the split yellow peas should both be soft. If they still have a little bite, cook for another 5–10 minutes – you want them to be completely soft, so that this dish is very easy to digest. If the mixture starts to catch on the base of the pan, add a splash of water.

3 > Stir through the spinach, along with a big spoonful of the coconut yogurt. Add the lemon or lime juice and season well. Add a splash of water if it seems a little thick.

4 > Spoon into 4 bowls and top each one with a spoonful of coconut yogurt. Scatter with the coriander and serve with the lemon or lime wedges.

4

A LITTLE
(OR A LOT!)
OF SPICE

STICKY FIVE-SPICE AUBERGINE AND RICE

Sweet, salty and sticky, all under one roof. This is a one-pan version of my favourite sticky Chinese aubergines. I love topping this dish with crispy fried onions, mainly because they're the best snack to tuck into while you're making dinner, but peanuts are just as delicious if you can't get hold of the crispy onions.

2 aubergines, cut into large bite-sized chunks

2 tablespoons coconut, vegetable or olive oil

1 tablespoon clear honey

1 tablespoon soy sauce

1 tablespoon white wine vinegar

bunch of spring onions, sliced

1 garlic clove, grated

thumb-sized piece of fresh root ginger, grated

1 teaspoon five spice powder

big pinch of dried chilli flakes

250 g (9 oz) pouch ready-cooked white rice

1 lime, ½ juiced and ½ cut into wedges

sea salt and freshly ground black pepper

sesame seeds or crispy onions, to serve

1 > Heat a large non-stick frying pan over a high heat. Once the pan is hot, add the aubergine chunks and dry-fry for 5 minutes until the aubergine is lightly charred. Season with salt, then add 1 tablespoon of oil along with 100 ml (3½ fl oz) water. Cover the pan with a lid and cook for 5 minutes more, until the water has evaporated and the aubergines are frying in the oil.

2 > Meanwhile, in a small jug, mix together the honey, soy sauce and vinegar, along with 1 tablespoon water. Set aside until needed.

3 > Remove the lid from the pan. Still over a high heat, add 1 tablespoon oil, along with half the spring onions. Stir, then add the garlic and ginger. Add the five spice powder and chilli flakes, then cook for 1 minute more. It should smell really fragrant. Reduce the heat to medium–low and pour the vinegar mix into the pan. Stir to coat the aubergines in the sticky sauce, and season to taste.

4 > Push the aubergine mixture to one side of the pan, or remove from the pan and set aside on a plate. Scrunch the rice pouch in your hands to break up the rice, then tip the contents into the opposite side of the pan, along with a big splash of water. Mix most of the remaining spring onions into the rice, along with the lime juice. Season well and warm through.

5 > Spoon the rice into 2 bowls and top with the aubergine mixture, then scatter with the reserved spring onions and sesame seeds or crispy onions. Serve with lime wedges.

POTATO AND PEA MASSAMAN CURRY

While not a traditional massaman, this curry is full of tricks to capture the flavour without the time and effort. Increase the peanut butter by another tablespoon if you're a fan of a super nutty flavour – I usually am! Serve with some warm naan bread.

1 tablespoon olive oil or coconut oil

1 onion, roughly chopped

1 teaspoon mixed spice

1 teaspoon ground cumin

1 teaspoon coriander seeds

3 tablespoons massaman or Thai red curry paste (if you're vegetarian/vegan, check the ingredients)

750 g (1 lb 10 oz) baby potatoes, halved

400 ml (14 fl oz) can coconut milk

1 vegetable stock cube

1 teaspoon caster or light brown sugar

2 tablespoons peanut butter

300 g (10½ oz) frozen peas

100 g (3½ oz) spinach

juice of 1 lime

sea salt and freshly ground black pepper

To serve
finely sliced green chilli
freshly chopped coriander

1 > Heat the oil in the base of a large saucepan over a medium–high heat. Add the onion, along with a big pinch of salt, and fry for about 5 minutes until softened. Add the mixed spice, cumin and coriander seeds and cook for 2 minutes further, then add the curry paste and stir well. Tip the potatoes into the pan and stir to coat in the spice mix.

2 > Pour in the coconut milk, then refill the emptied can with water and pour that into the pan too. Add the stock cube and bring to the boil. Bubble for 10–12 minutes, until the sauce has thickened and the potatoes are cooked. You can test them with a sharp knife: it should slide right through.

3 > Stir in the sugar and peanut butter, then add the peas, spinach and lime juice. Taste and season. Bring to the boil, stirring, to wilt the spinach and quickly defrost the peas.

4 > To serve, spoon the curry into bowls and top with the sliced green chilli and freshly chopped coriander.

SPICED COD AND BUTTER BEANS
WITH AIOLI

This has the vibe of paella, but it's quicker and simpler. You'll need to salt the cod before you cook it. If you can do it a day in advance, it'll be delicious, but even half an hour will make a difference. Serve with a green salad and bread.

4 chunky cod fillets, about 150 g (5¼ oz) each
1 tablespoon olive oil
2 large red peppers, cored, deseeded and cut into strips
2 shallots or 1 onion, finely chopped
1 stock cube (fish, chicken or vegetable)
big pinch of saffron (optional)
1 garlic clove, finely sliced
2 teaspoons smoked paprika
125 ml (4 fl oz) white wine
2 x 400 g (14 oz) cans butter beans
small bunch of parsley, roughly chopped
sea salt and freshly ground black pepper
½ lemon, cut into wedges, to serve

For the aioli
½ garlic clove
4 tablespoons mayonnaise
juice of ½ lemon

1 > Start by salting the cod. Place the fillets on a plate and sprinkle over 2 teaspoons salt, rubbing it into the flesh. Transfer to the refrigerator until you're ready to cook. You can do this up to a day in advance.

2 > When you're ready to cook, heat the olive oil in a large non-stick frying pan over a medium–high heat. Add the peppers and shallots or onion, along with a big pinch of salt. Fry for 8–10 minutes until completely soft.

3 > Meanwhile, put the stock cube into a measuring jug, along with the saffron, if using. Add 500ml boiling water and stir so the stock cube dissolves. Then make the aioli. Grate the garlic into a bowl with the mayonnaise. Add the lemon juice, stir and season.

4 > Add the garlic slices to the frying pan, along with the paprika. Stir well to coat the vegetables and cook for 1 minute more. Add the white wine and bring to the boil, then pour in the stock.

5 > Drain and rinse the contents of one of the cans of butter beans. Add the rinsed butter beans to the frying pan, then tip the contents of the other can into the pan too (including the liquid this time). Stir in most of the chopped parsley. Bring to the boil, then reduce the heat to a simmer and cook until the liquid has thickened a little.

6 > Nestle the cod fillets into the beans and cook for 3–5 minutes until the fillets are cooked through and flaking apart.

7 > Scatter over the remaining parsley and divide between 4 plates, adding a dollop of aioli and a lemon wedge to each one.

Photograph overleaf >

KERALAN PRAWN CURRY

You'll make this once and it'll instantly go on your list of recipes that you can roll out time and time again. The ingredients are things you tend to have in the cupboard or refrigerator already, and you can swap out the prawns for more veggies or some white fish.

250 g (9 oz) rice (jasmine or basmati)

1 tablespoon coconut, vegetable or olive oil

1 red chilli, finely chopped

small bunch of spring onions, finely sliced

thumb-sized piece of fresh root ginger, grated

1 garlic clove, grated

2 teaspoons ground turmeric

2 teaspoons medium curry powder

400 ml (14 fl oz) can coconut milk

250 g (9 oz) cherry tomatoes

300 g (10½ oz) raw prawns

125 g (4½ oz) spinach

1 lime, ½ juiced and ½ cut into wedges

sea salt and freshly ground black pepper

1 > Place the rice in a sieve and rinse really well with cold water – this stops it clumping. Set aside.

2 > Heat the oil in a large saucepan over a medium heat. Add the chilli and most of the spring onions, followed by the ginger and garlic. Add a big pinch of salt and fry until everything is softened. Add the turmeric and curry powder and fry for 2 minutes further – this cooks the spices and stops them tasting raw.

3 > Tip the rinsed rice into the pan and stir well. Pour in the coconut milk, then refill the emptied can with water and pour that into the pan too. Bring the mixture to the boil, then add the cherry tomatoes and reduce the heat right down to low. Cover and simmer for 15 minutes. Don't stir – stirring causes the rice to turn mushy!

4 > Once the rice is almost cooked, add the prawns, spinach and lime juice. Stir and cook for 2 minutes further.

5 > Season well and serve topped with the remaining spring onions and the lime wedges.

MUSHROOM AND AUBERGINE CURRY
WITH BROWN RICE

I love brown food and this is no exception. It's warm and indulgent, while also feeling fresh and healthy. You can serve the rice on the side if you prefer, but I love stirring it into the curry, then spooning it into bowls and digging in. The mango chutney is optional, but I think you'll regret not adding a big dollop.

2 aubergines, cut into 3 cm (1¼ inch) chunks

1 tablespoon olive oil

350 g (12 oz) mushrooms (use any mix of mushrooms you like), sliced, small ones kept whole

1 onion, finely sliced

1 green chilli, finely sliced

1 garlic clove, grated

thumb-sized piece of fresh root ginger, grated

2 teaspoons ground turmeric

1 teaspoon black mustard seeds (optional)

1 tablespoon medium curry powder

400 ml (14 fl oz) can coconut milk

1 lime, ½ juiced and ½ cut into wedges

2 x 250 g (9 oz) pouches ready-cooked brown or wholegrain rice

sea salt and freshly ground black pepper

To serve
nigella seeds
mango chutney (optional)

1 > Heat a large non-stick, high-sided frying pan over a high heat. Add the aubergine chunks and dry-fry for 6–8 minutes, until starting to char, shaking the pan regularly.

2 > Reduce the heat a little. Add the olive oil to the pan, along with the mushrooms and onion. Fry, stirring occasionally, for around 10 more minutes, until the vegetables have softened. If anything starts to stick, add a splash of water to the pan.

3 > Add most of the green chilli, along with the garlic and ginger. Stir in the turmeric, mustard seeds, if using, and curry powder and cook for 2 more minutes. Pour the coconut milk into the pan, then half-fill the emptied can with water and pour that into the pan too. Cook for 10 minutes until the sauce has thickened.

4 > Season well and add the lime juice. Stir the rice pouches into the curry. Top with the remaining green chilli and a scattering of nigella seeds, if using. Serve with a dollop of mango chutney and the lime wedges.

SAAG AND MATAR PANEER

I've never been great at choosing between two good things, and this dish is a bit of an ode to that side of myself. I love saag paneer and I love matar paneer – so instead of choosing between them, I combined them! Now you can enjoy the joy of both spinach AND peas with your paneer. If you can't find paneer, halloumi is a great (untraditional) alternative.

500 g (1 lb 2 oz) baby leaf spinach

2 tablespoons coconut, vegetable or olive oil

1 teaspoon ground turmeric

1 teaspoon chilli powder

450 g (1 lb) paneer, cut into 2 cm (¾ inch) cubes

1 onion, finely chopped

1 green chilli, deseeded if you don't like spice, finely chopped

1 garlic clove, grated

thumb-sized piece of fresh root ginger, grated

1 teaspoon garam masala

200 g (7 oz) frozen peas

juice of ½ lemon

sea salt

naan bread, to serve (optional)

1 > Place the spinach in a colander or sieve. Pour boiling water over the spinach to wilt it down. Set aside until cool enough to handle.

2 > Meanwhile, in a large bowl, mix together the oil, ground turmeric and chilli powder. Add the paneer cubes, season well with salt and toss so the cubes are well coated.

3 > Heat a large non-stick frying pan over a medium–high heat and tip the spiced paneer into the pan. Fry for 5–8 minutes until golden and crisp, turning regularly.

4 > While the paneer is cooking, tip the wilted spinach into a clean tea towel and draw in the edges of the towel to create a parcel. Hold it over the sink and twist to squeeze out as much moisture as you possibly can.

5 > Use a pair of tongs to transfer the cooked paneer back to the bowl. Add the onion and green chilli to the pan. There should be enough oil left in the pan from frying the paneer, but add a little more if needed. Season well with salt, then add the garlic, ginger and garam masala. Stir and toast for a couple of minutes: this will stop the dish tasting of raw spice.

6 > Tip the frozen peas into the pan, along with the spinach, and toss. Add a splash of water to release anything stuck to the base of the pan. Once everything is heated through and any water has evaporated, return the paneer to the pan and toss to combine. Squeeze over the lemon juice, then serve straight from the pan, with warm naan bread on the side, if you like.

CURRIED CARROT LENTILS
WITH LIME YOGURT

Sweet, sticky, spicy carrots served with puy lentils, this dish is sure
to be a treat for veggies and meat-eaters alike.

1 tablespoon salted butter

2 teaspoons medium curry
powder

6 medium-sized carrots, sliced
in half lengthways (no need
to peel!)

400 ml (14 fl oz) vegetable stock

4 tablespoons natural yogurt

juice of 1 lime

1 tablespoon clear honey

250 g (9 oz) pouch pre-cooked
puy lentils

sea salt and freshly ground black
pepper

To serve
freshly chopped coriander
toasted flaked almonds or
coconut flakes

1 > Heat the butter in a large non-stick, high-sided frying pan over a
medium–high heat. Once the butter has melted and is foaming, add
the curry powder and stir to combine. Place the carrots in the pan,
cut-side down, in as even a layer as you can. Cover with the lid and
cook for 5 minutes, until the carrots are charred on their flat sides.

2 > Season the stock with salt and pepper, then pour it into the pan.
It should come to about halfway up the carrots. You can add a little
more water if you need to. Put the lid back on and cook for another
12–15 minutes, until a knife slides easily into the centre of the carrots.

3 > Meanwhile, in a small bowl, mix together the yogurt and half the lime
juice. Season well and set aside until needed.

4 > Remove the lid from the pan and drizzle in the honey. Toss the carrots
in the sauce and let it all bubble away for 5 minutes, stirring regularly,
until the carrots are well coated and the sauce is thick and sticky. Add
the lentils and stir. Cook for 2–3 minutes until the lentils are warmed
through. Add the remaining lime juice and season well.

5> To serve, top the curried carrot lentils with a drizzle of the lime yogurt.
Scatter over the chopped coriander and flaked almonds or coconut
flakes and enjoy.

BEST-EVER CHICKPEA CURRY

You can use a can of tomatoes here if you would prefer, but I love the lightness that fresh tomatoes bring. It's all about cooking them for a while, with a pinch of sugar, to really bring all their flavour to the party. To make this dish suitable for vegans, just leave out the yogurt when serving.

2 x 400 g (14 oz) cans chickpeas

1 vegetable stock cube

1 tablespoon vegetable, coconut
or olive oil

2 onions, finely chopped

2 garlic cloves, grated

thumb-sized piece of fresh root
ginger, grated

2 green chillies, 1 finely chopped
and 1 finely sliced, deseeded if
you don't like spice

1 teaspoon ground cumin

1 teaspoon ground coriander

1 teaspoon garam masala

1 teaspoon ground turmeric

6 large tomatoes, roughly
chopped

1 teaspoon caster or light brown
sugar

juice of ½ lemon

sea salt and freshly ground black
pepper

To serve

freshly chopped coriander

natural yogurt

naan bread

1 > Tip the contents of the cans or jar of chickpeas, including the liquid, into a bowl and add 350 ml (12 fl oz) boiling water and the stock cube. Stir well to make sure the stock cube has dissolved.

2 > Heat the oil in a large saucepan over a medium–high heat. Add the onion, along with a big pinch of salt, and fry for around 5 minutes, stirring regularly, until the onion has softened. Add the garlic, ginger and finely chopped green chilli and fry for 3–4 minutes further.

3 > Stir in the spices and toast for a couple of minutes: this will stop your curry tasting of raw spice. Add the chopped tomatoes, along with the sugar and a big splash of water, and cook for 15 minutes, stirring regularly and smushing the tomatoes.

4 > Add the chickpea and stock mixture. Reduce the heat to medium–low and simmer for 30 minutes.

5 > Season the curry with salt and pepper, and stir through the lemon juice. Split between 4 bowls and scatter over the fresh coriander and sliced green chilli. Serve with cooling yogurt and naan bread.

CAULIFLOWER KORMA

*If you're after a great weeknight veggie dish, let this be your new staple.
It's a little bit of a treat, but using natural yogurt rather than cream makes
it a lighter option.*

50 g (1¾ oz) ground almonds
1 tablespoon olive, coconut or
  vegetable oil
1 large or 2 small cauliflowers
  (about 1 kg/2 lb 4 oz), cut into
  medium-sized florets
2 onions, sliced
2 garlic cloves, grated
thumb-sized piece of fresh root
  ginger, grated
2 teaspoons garam masala
pinch of dried chilli flakes
2 teaspoons tomato puree
2 teaspoons clear honey
1 vegetable stock cube
300 ml (10 fl oz) natural yogurt
60 g (2¼ oz) sultanas or raisins
sea salt and freshly ground black
  pepper

To serve
toasted flaked almonds
freshly chopped coriander
rice (optional)

1 > Place the ground almonds in a large saucepan over a medium–high heat. Toast them for a couple of minutes, stirring constantly, until they are brown and smell really nutty. Tip into a bowl and set aside.

2 > Return the saucepan to the heat and add the oil. Add the cauliflower florets and cook for 5 minutes, stirring regularly, then add the onions. Fry for 10 minutes, until the cauliflower and onions are softening and charring in places. Add the garlic and ginger. Fry for a couple more minutes, then add the garam masala and chilli flakes and toast for 1 minute longer, stirring them into the veg mix. Frying the spices like this will ensure your curry doesn't taste of raw spice.

3 > Add the tomato puree and stir, then drizzle in the honey. Crumble in the stock cube and pour over 350 ml (12 fl oz) water. Bring to the boil and stir to make sure the stock cube has dissolved. Now add the natural yogurt, toasted ground almonds and sultanas or raisins, and season well. Cook for 10 minutes, until the vegetables are cooked through. Check them for doneness: if the cauliflower is still a little firm, simmer for 5 minutes further.

4 > Divide the korma between 4 bowls and top with the toasted flaked almonds and freshly chopped coriander. Serve with rice, if you like.

SWEET POTATO, KALE AND CASHEW CURRY

This dish is a beauty, because it's so impressive and flavour-packed, but it honestly takes very little effort. I serve this curry with a big dollop of cooling yogurt, but you can leave that out to make it vegan.

1 tablespoon olive, coconut or sesame oil

bunch of spring onions, finely sliced

2 garlic cloves, grated

thumb-sized piece of fresh root ginger, grated

3–4 tablespoons Thai red curry paste (depending on the strength of the paste – and if you are vegetarian, don't forget to check the ingredients)

400 ml (14 fl oz) can coconut milk

1 tablespoon cashew butter or peanut butter

500 g (1 lb 2 oz) sweet potatoes, chopped into bite-sized chunks

150 g (5¼ oz) kale, torn into bite-sized pieces

juice of 1 lime

handful of roasted cashews, roughly chopped

sea salt and freshly ground black pepper

To serve
Greek yogurt
naan bread (optional)

1 > Heat the oil in a large saucepan over a medium–high heat. Add most of the spring onions, along with a big pinch of salt, and fry for 2 minutes. Add the garlic and ginger, fry for 2 minutes more, then add the Thai red curry paste. Fry, stirring, for a further 2 minutes, then tip the coconut milk into the pan. Refill the emptied can three-quarters full of water, and pour that into the pan too. Add the cashew or peanut butter and stir well to combine.

2 > Bring to the boil, then add the sweet potato chunks. Reduce the heat to low and simmer away for 20–25 minutes until the sweet potato is cooked through. Add the kale and lime juice, stir well to combine and cook for 1–2 minutes, until the kale is wilted. Season well with salt and pepper.

3 > Spoon the curry into bowls. Scatter over the chopped cashews and the remaining spring onion. Serve with a dollop of Greek yogurt, if using, in each bowl, with some naan bread on the side, if you like.

BUTTERNUT AND CAULIFLOWER DHAL

I've spent a lot of time making and eating different dhals. This one uses coconut milk, which is a little untraditional, but always adds an extra level of satisfaction for me. This is also a great option to batch cook and eat on repeat, as it gets better every day!

1 tablespoon coconut, sunflower or olive oil

500 g (1 lb 2 oz) butternut squash, peeled and chopped into 3 cm (1¼ inch) chunks

1 onion, finely chopped

1 small cauliflower, or ½ large, cut into florets, leaves reserved and sliced

1 garlic clove, grated

1 green chilli, finely chopped

thumb-sized piece of fresh root ginger, grated

1 heaped teaspoon ground cumin

1 heaped teaspoon ground coriander

2 teaspoons ground turmeric

200 g (7 oz) red split lentils

400 ml (14 fl oz) can coconut milk

1 vegetable stock cube

juice of 1 lemon or lime

sea salt and freshly ground black pepper

To serve

natural yogurt

freshly chopped coriander

coconut flakes

1 > Heat the oil in a large saucepan over a medium–high heat. Add the squash and fry for 10 minutes until beginning to brown.

2 > Add the onion and cauliflower florets to the pan and fry for 5 minutes, then add the garlic, chilli and ginger. Stir well, then add the spices and stir to coat all the veggies. Add the lentils, followed by the coconut milk and the vegetable stock cube. Refill the emptied can with water and pour that into the pan too. Season with salt and pepper and bring to the boil, stirring to ensure the stock cube has dissolved.

3 > Reduce the heat to medium–low and add the sliced cauliflower leaves. Cover with a lid and simmer for 20 minutes, checking halfway through and adding a little extra water if it looks too thick. Remove the lid and simmer for another 5 minutes, stirring. The lentils should be completely soft .

4 > Squeeze the lemon or lime juice into the pan, then taste and season. Allow to cool and relax a little, then spoon the dhal into 4 bowls and top with a dollop of yogurt and a scattering of fresh coriander and coconut flakes.

5
WEEK-ENDERS AND FAKE-AWAYS

FRYING PAN GRANOLA
WITH QUICK FRUIT COMPOTE

If you've run out of granola, why not make your own? Once it's cooked, try to put the pan outside if you can, so the granola can cool down and crisp up at super speed. You can serve it with fresh fruit and yogurt, or make a quick warm compote as I have done here.

100 g (3½ oz) rolled oats

75 g (2½ oz) mixed nuts (I like hazelnuts, walnut and pecans), roughly chopped

2 tablespoons mixed seeds (I like pumpkin and sunflower seeds)

2 tablespoons desiccated coconut

1 teaspoon ground cinnamon

3 tablespoons olive oil

4 tablespoons maple syrup (or golden syrup)

250 g (9 oz) frozen summer fruits

sea salt

300 ml (10 fl oz) natural or Greek yogurt, to serve

1 > Line a baking sheet with baking paper and place it in the refrigerator until needed. Mix the oats, mixed nuts, seeds, coconut and cinnamon together in a bowl. Add a pinch of salt.

2 > Pour the oil and 3 tablespoons of the maple syrup into a large frying pan over a medium heat and whisk together a little – don't worry if they don't fully combine. Tip the oat mixture into the frying pan and stir well so that everything is coated in the oil and syrup mix. Reduce the heat to low and cook for 15–20 minutes, stirring regularly, until the mixture is golden.

3 > Transfer the mixture to the prepared cold baking sheet. Spread the granola out, then set aside to cool and crisp up. This will work even better if you are able to place it outside to cool down at speed.

4 > Wipe the pan, then tip in the frozen fruit and the remaining maple syrup. Place the pan over a medium–high heat and simmer for 10 minutes, until syrupy. Allow to cool slightly (or chill in the refrigerator if you would prefer the compote to be cool).

5 > To serve, divide the yogurt between 4 bowls and top with the compote and granola.

HARISSA BAKED EGGS WITH SWEET POTATO

Brunch, sorted. This dish can easily be made suitable for vegetarians by simply omitting the chorizo.

1 tablespoon olive oil

1 sweet potato (around 200 g/ 7 oz), cut into 2 cm (¾ inch) chunks

2 red peppers, cored, deseeded and sliced into 1 cm (½ inch) strips

2 red onions, sliced into chunky wedges

150g (5¼ oz) chorizo, sliced at an angle

2 garlic cloves, grated

3 tablespoons harissa paste

400 g (14 oz) can chopped tomatoes

400 g (14 oz) can cannellini beans

juice of 1 lemon

8 eggs

sea salt and freshly ground black pepper

To serve

75 ml (2½ fl oz) natural yogurt

roasted nuts (I use almonds)

small bunch of fresh chives, chopped

toast or chunky bread

1 > Heat the olive oil in a large non-stick frying pan over a medium–high heat. Add the sweet potato and red peppers, along with a big pinch of salt, and fry for 8–10 minutes until beginning to soften.

2 > Add the red onions and the chorizo slices and gently fry for 5 minutes further, adding a splash of water if they start to stick at all. Now add the garlic and stir in the harissa paste.

3 > Add the chopped tomatoes to the pan. Half-fill the emptied can with water and pour that into the pan too. Bring to the boil, then reduce the heat to medium and let it bubble away for 15–20 minutes, until the vegetables are cooked through. You can test them by poking them with a knife: it should slide through. Tip the cannellini beans in, along with the liquid from their can. Stir well and bring to the boil. Simmer for 5 minutes, until the mixture has thickened. Stir in the lemon juice and season well.

4 > Use a spatula or spoon to create an egg-sized hole in the mixture and crack an egg into the hollow. Repeat with the remaining eggs. Don't worry if they spill out a bit: the beauty is in the mess! Cover with a lid and cook for 8–10 minutes, until the egg whites have set but the yolks are still soft. Remove the lid and leave to stand off the heat for 1 minute to relax before serving.

5 > Top with dollops of yogurt and scatter over the nuts and chives. Serve immediately with toast or chunky bread for mopping up the sauce.

GIANT BACON AND EGG HASH BROWN

You don't need many ingredients to make a winning breakfast and this proves the point. Serve with your favourite breakfast condiment: I love sriracha or HP sauce. Using scissors to snip the chives is a real game-changer.

4 medium floury potatoes (about 400 g/14 oz in total), coarsely grated, skin left on
1 onion, very finely sliced
1 tablespoon olive oil
160 g (5¾ oz) diced pancetta
4 eggs
sea salt and freshly ground black pepper

To serve
fresh chives
condiments of your choice

1 > Place the grated potato in a sieve and rinse well in cold water to remove some of the starch. Lay a clean tea towel out on a clean kitchen surface, and place the potato and onion in the middle of the towel. Draw together the corners to make a parcel, then twist it over the sink to squeeze out as much water as you can. Tip onto a plate and pat dry with kitchen roll. You want the mixture to be as dry as possible!

2 > Heat the olive oil in a large frying pan over a medium–high heat. Add the diced pancetta and fry for 2–3 minutes, until starting to colour. Add the potato and onion mixture to the pan and fry for 12–15 minutes, stirring regularly so the potato gets golden and crispy in places.

3 > Create 4 egg-sized holes in the potato mixture. Crack an egg into each and fry for 3 minutes, then cover with a lid and cook for around 2 minutes further or until the egg whites have set. Remove the lid and season with salt and pepper. Use scissors to finely snip the chives over the top, and serve with condiments galore.

KATSU CURRY

*This really needs no introduction. It's your favourite takeaway curry,
in one-pan format. You. Are. Welcome.*

2 tablespoons coconut or olive
    oil, plus extra if needed
2 tablespoons breadcrumbs
    (I use panko)
1 small onion, sliced
1 garlic clove, grated
thumb-sized piece of fresh root
    ginger, grated
1 teaspoon ground turmeric
2 teaspoons medium curry
    powder
2 skinless and boneless chicken
    breasts, about 150 g (5½ oz)
    each
150 g (5½ oz) basmati rice, rinsed
    with cold water
400 ml (14 fl oz) can coconut milk
1 tablespoon soy sauce
2 teaspoons caster sugar
juice of 1 lime
sea salt

To serve
freshly chopped coriander
lime wedges

1 > First, make your crispy breadcrumbs. Heat about 1 tablespoon oil in
a large non-stick, high-sided frying pan over a medium heat. Add the
breadcrumbs and fry for 3–5 minutes until crisp and golden. Tip into
a bowl and set aside.

2 > Return the pan to the heat and raise the heat to medium–high. Add
1 tablespoon oil. Once hot, add the onion, along with a big pinch of
salt. Fry gently for around 5 minutes, until softened. Add the garlic and
ginger and stir. Cook for 2 more minutes, then add the turmeric and
curry powder and cook for 1 minute longer. Add a splash of water if
the mixture starts to catch on the base of the pan.

3 > Add the chicken breasts, along with a splash more oil if needed, and
stir to coat in the spicy mix. Cook for 1 minute, then add the rice. Stir
to coat, then pour in the coconut milk, along with the soy sauce and
sugar, and stir well. Bring to the boil, then reduce the heat to low, cover
with a lid and simmer for 15 minutes.

4 > Remove from the heat and stir in the lime juice. Scatter over the
crispy breadcrumbs and coriander and serve with the lime wedges.

Tip >
If you want to present this dish in a more traditional katsu style, remove
the chicken breasts from the pan and slice them before serving.

BACON BAKED BEANS

*Load these beans into a baked potato or spoon on to a slice of toast.
This dish will taste even better after a good night's sleep – so save any
leftovers to enjoy tomorrow!*

1 tablespoon olive oil

120 g (4¼ oz) diced pancetta

1 red onion, finely sliced

2 celery sticks, sliced into 3 mm
  (⅛ inch) slices

1 garlic, finely sliced

1 teaspoon smoked paprika

200 g (7 oz) cherry tomatoes

1 tablespoon tomato puree

1 tablespoon light brown sugar

400 ml (14 fl oz) can passata
  (sieved tomatoes)

2 x 400 g (14 oz) cans cannellini or
  butter beans

Worcestershire sauce, optional

sea salt and freshly ground black
  pepper

1 > Heat half a tablespoon olive oil in a large, high-sided, non-stick frying
pan over a medium–high heat, and add the diced pancetta. Fry for
6–8 minutes until crisp, then move to a plate lined with kitchen roll,
leaving the juices in the pan.

2 > Keeping the pan over the same heat, add the onion and celery, along
with a pinch of salt, and fry for 5 minutes until softened. Add the garlic
and fry for 2 minutes further, then add the smoked paprika. Stir well
to coat everything, then add the cherry tomatoes, along with the
remaining oil. Fry for about 3 minutes until the tomato skins start
to burst, then stir in the tomato puree and brown sugar. Next, pour
the passata into the pan. Bring to the boil, then tip the cans of beans
into the pan, including their liquid. Bring to the boil again, then reduce
the heat to medium. Season well and simmer for 10–15 minutes,
stirring regularly.

3 > Splash in some Worcestershire sauce, if using, then scatter over the
crispy bacon. Serve on top of toast, with a dollop of yogurt, or piled
into a baked potato: the options are endless!

ALL-IN-ONE CARBONARA

Forget everything you may have been taught about carbonara – this is the best way to make it. There's no need to worry about split sauce, because here we cook it all in one pan and use the remaining pasta water to make the most perfect silky sauce. But don't take my word for it: give it a go and you'll never make carbonara another way again.

½ tablespoon olive oil
120 g (4¼ oz) diced pancetta
1 garlic clove, peeled and bashed, but left whole
200 g (7 oz) dried spaghetti
1 egg plus 2 extra egg yolks
40 g (1½ oz) Parmesan cheese, finely grated
sea salt and freshly ground black pepper

1 > Heat the olive oil in a large non-stick, high-sided frying pan over a medium–high heat. Add the diced pancetta and fry for 5–6 minutes until crisp.

2 > Remove the pancetta from the pan with a slotted spoon and set aside on a plate. Keeping the pan on the heat, add the garlic clove and press it into the oil in the pan. Fry for 1 minute, until a little golden, then add the spaghetti to the pan along with 600 ml (20 fl oz) boiling water. You might have to break up your spaghetti a bit if the pan is too small for it to fit. Cover with a lid and bring to the boil. Cook for 10–11 minutes.

3 > Meanwhile, in a small bowl or jug, whisk the whole egg and egg yolks well until no streaks remain, then whisk in three-quarters of the Parmesan and a big pinch of salt and pepper.

4 > After 10–11 minutes of cooking, the pasta should be cooked but still have a very slight bite. Remove the lid of the frying pan and turn off the heat. There will still be some water in the pan with the pasta. Don't worry: this will become your amazing sauce! Very slowly pour the egg-and-Parmesan mixture into the pan, holding a pair of tongs in your other hand and using them to stir everything together. As you stir, the water and egg mixture will combine into a beautiful silky sauce. Return the pancetta to the pan, toss to combine, and season generously with black pepper.

5 > Use the tongs to divide the pasta between 2 bowls. Finish by sprinkling over the remaining Parmesan and serve with another crack of black pepper.

Photograph overleaf >

CHICKEN WINGS

I bet you never thought you could make the most delicious, sticky, crispy chicken wings on the stove top. Allow me to prove you wrong.

500 g (1 lb 2 oz) chicken wings
2 tablespoons cornflour
2 tablespoons vegetable oil
1 tablespoon clear honey
1 tablespoon soy sauce
2 tablespoons tomato ketchup
1 tablespoon sriracha
1 garlic clove, grated
thumb-sized piece of fresh root
    ginger, grated
sea salt and freshly ground black
    pepper

To serve
finely sliced spring onions
toasted sesame seeds

1 > Toss the chicken wings in a large bowl with the cornflour and a large pinch of salt and pepper to coat.

2 > Heat the oil in a large non-stick frying pan over a medium–high heat. Make sure the oil is really hot before you add all the wings to the pan. Just add one to begin with, to test: it should sizzle as soon as it hits the oil. Once you're confident the oil is hot enough, add all the chicken wings to the pan and fry for 8–10 minutes, turning halfway, until crisp.

3 > Meanwhile, in another large bowl, whisk together the honey, soy sauce, tomato ketchup and sriracha. Add the garlic and ginger and season with salt and pepper, then mix well to combine.

4 > When the chicken wings are cooked through and crisp, use a pair of tongs to lift them out of the pan and into the bowl of sauce. Toss so they are completely coated in the sauce.

5 > Carefully drain the oil from the pan and wipe it clean with some kitchen roll. Tip the wings and sauce back into the wiped pan and cook over a low heat for 5 minutes or until the sauce is reduced to a sticky glaze. Top with the spring onions and sesame seeds to serve.

LAMB FLATBREAD PIZZA

Instead of making a pizza dough, this cheat makes use of flatbreads as a base. You can so easily change this up, using pork, beef or soy mince, and switching the tzatziki for hummus or baba ganoush. It's perfect for a super-speedy supper, or a great option for a working-from-home lunch treat.

2 tablespoons olive oil

2 red onions, finely chopped

juice of 1 lemon

200 g (7 oz) cherry tomatoes, halved

250 g (9 oz) lamb mince (use mince with a high fat percentage for extra flavour)

1 garlic clove, grated

1 teaspoon ground coriander

1 teaspoon ground cumin

2 flatbreads

4 tablespoons ready-made tzatziki

sea salt and freshly ground black pepper

To serve

fresh mint leaves

toasted flaked almonds

1 > Heat 1 tablespoon oil in a large non-stick frying pan over a medium heat. Add three-quarters of the chopped red onion, along with a pinch of salt, and fry for about 5 minutes until softened.

2 > Meanwhile, put the remaining chopped red onion in a small bowl with the lemon juice and 1 tablespoon olive oil. Add the cherry tomatoes to the bowl and toss well. Season with salt and pepper and set aside.

3 > Once the onions in the pan have softened, increase the heat to high and add the lamb mince. Fry for about 8 minutes, stirring regularly, until the mince is brown and beginning to crisp up.

4 > Add the garlic, along with the ground coriander and cumin. Stir and cook for 2 minutes, then tip the mixture into a clean bowl and set aside until needed, keeping some of the juices in the pan.

5 > Keeping the pan over the heat, toss the flatbreads into the pan to heat through in the lamb juices. Fry for around 2 minutes on each side until charred.

6 > To serve, spread half the tzatziki over each flatbread and top with the crispy lamb mix. Scatter over the tomato and onion salad, then finish with fresh mint leaves and toasted flaked almonds. Use scissors to cut the pizza into slices.

PULLED PORK NACHOS

This is the perfect dish for having friends over. First, you can make the pork in advance and reheat it when it's time to eat, ready to be served with all the toppings. Secondly, you could make some homemade guac if you want to show off. Thirdly, you can plonk it on the middle of the table and people can spoon it into their bowls or eat it directly from the pan.

1 tablespoon olive oil
800 g (1 lb 12 oz) pork shoulder, diced
1 red onion, finely chopped
2 garlic cloves, grated
2 teaspoons smoked paprika
2 teaspoons ground cumin
1 tablespoon light or dark brown sugar
200 ml (7 fl oz) cider or beer
1 stock cube (vegetable or chicken)
2 x 400 g (14 oz) cans black beans or kidney beans
100 g (3½ oz) Cheddar cheese, grated
180 g (6½ oz) tortilla chips
sea salt and freshly ground black pepper

To serve
guacamole
soured cream
sliced jalapeños from a jar

1 > Heat the olive oil in a large non-stick high-sided frying pan or saucepan over a high heat. Once hot, add the diced pork shoulder. Season and cook for around 3 minutes, until brown. Reduce the heat to medium and add the red onion. Fry gently for a couple of minutes, until starting to soften, then add the garlic, paprika, cumin and brown sugar. Stir to combine, then add the cider or beer, along with 400 ml (14 fl oz) water and the stock cube.

2 > Reduce the heat to very low. Cover the pan with a sheet of tin foil, then top with the lid to hold the tin foil down. Cook for 1 hour, then remove the foil and lid and cook gently for 2 hours more, until the pork is melting apart. You will know when the pork is done, as it will fall apart when prodded.

3 > Use two forks to shred the meat in the pan. If you find it easier, you can lift the meat out of the pan and shred it on a plate or board, then return to the pan. Add the beans, along with the liquid from their cans, and season well. Increase the heat to medium–high and cook for 20 minutes, until the sauce has reduced. Remove from the heat and allow to rest for 5 minutes so the pork can soak up some of the juices.

4 > Scatter the cheese over the pork and beans mix, then top with a handful of the tortilla chips, digging a few of them into the cheesy pork. You only need to add enough to just cover the top; you can serve remaining tortilla chips on the side for people to tuck in to at the table. Return the pan to the heat and cook for 5 minutes further, until the cheese has begun to melt.

5 > Dollop the guacamole, soured cream and sliced jalapeños on top and serve, or put them in bowls for people to help themselves to.

BREAKFAST TACOS

It's messy work, and if you come away without any spillages and clean hands, then you didn't do it right. Make sure to wrap the tacos in a clean tea towel as soon as you have cooked them, otherwise they will dry out.

4 small taco tortillas (I love corn tortillas)
2 tablespoons olive oil
1 garlic clove, finely grated or crushed
½ green chilli, finely chopped
½ teaspoon ground coriander
100 g (3½ oz) greens, spinach or roughly chopped kale
4 eggs
sea salt and freshly ground black pepper

To serve
3 tablespoons Greek yogurt
25 g (1 oz) feta cheese
fresh coriander leaves
dried chilli flakes

1 > Heat a large non-stick frying pan over a high heat. Once it's super-hot, add the taco tortillas, one at a time. Cook each one for 30 seconds on each side, until charred. Once cooked, transfer the tacos to a clean tea towel, layering the cooked tacos on top of each other and wrapping them up in the tea towel as you go: this is the key to keeping them soft and warm. Set aside the tacos wrapped in the tea towel. Remove the pan from the heat to cool a little.

2 > Heat 1 tablespoon olive oil in the frying pan over a medium–high heat. Add the garlic, green chilli and ground coriander, along with a big pinch of salt, and fry for 2 minutes, until the garlic is golden. Add the greens and season with salt and pepper. Fry, stirring well, for 2–3 minutes more, until the greens are cooked. If the pan looks watery from the greens, keep stirring and frying until all the liquid has evaporated.

3 > Push the greens to one side of the pan, add the remaining oil to the opposite, empty side of the pan. Crack in the eggs and fry for around 3 minutes, until the whites have set. Don't worry about the greens catching a little on the base of the pan; it's nice to have a little char to them! When the eggs are cooked, remove the pan from the heat.

4 > To serve, spread the Greek yogurt on the tacos and top each one with the spicy greens, followed by a fried egg. Crumble the feta over the top and scatter with fresh coriander and chilli flakes. Pick up and attempt to eat without egg dribbling down your chin!

A KINDA AUBERGINE PARMIGIANA
WITH CRISPY BREADCRUMBS

Once you've made a parmigiana this way, you'll be hesitant to return to the traditional method. It's much more low maintenance and just as comforting. Use fresh or panko breadcrumbs, and make sure to fry them until really crisp!

2 tablespoons olive oil

4 tablespoons fresh or panko breadcrumbs

3 aubergines, chopped into 6 cm (2½ inch) chunks

1 red onion, finely sliced

1 garlic clove, finely sliced

1 tablespoon tomato puree

125 ml (4 fl oz) red wine

400 g (14 oz) can chopped tomatoes

250 g (9 oz) cherry tomatoes

1 tablespoon balsamic vinegar

2 x 125 g (4½ oz) balls mozzarella

25 g (1 oz) Parmesan cheese, finely grated

sea salt and freshly ground black pepper

fresh basil leaves, torn, to serve

1 > First, make your crispy breadcrumbs. Heat 1 tablespoon olive oil in a large non-stick, high-sided frying pan over a medium heat. Add the breadcrumbs and fry for 3–5 minutes until deep golden and crisp. Tip into a bowl and set aside.

2 > Return the frying pan to the heat. Over a high heat, add the aubergine chunks, along with a big pinch of salt (this helps the aubergines to release their water and cook faster). Fry for around 15 minutes until browning and collapsing, tossing the pan every now and then so the chunks can cook evenly. You may have to do this in batches.

3 > Reduce the heat a little. Add the onion and garlic to the pan along with the remaining olive oil. Cook for 3–4 minutes until the onions have softened, then add the tomato puree and stir to coat everything. Pour in the wine and bubble for about 2 minutes until reduced by half. Tip in the chopped tomatoes, along with the fresh cherry tomatoes. Reduce the heat to low and simmer for 10 minutes. If the mixture starts to catch on the base of the pan, add a splash of water.

4 > Stir in the balsamic vinegar, then taste the mixture and season with salt and pepper. Tear the mozzarella into big chunks and push them into the pan, nestling them into the tomato and aubergine mix. Increase the heat to medium–high, then scatter over the Parmesan. Cover with a lid and cook for a couple of minutes, until the mozzarella is gooey and the Parmesan has melted to make a cheesy layer.

5 > Allow to sit for a couple of minutes to settle the sauce. Scatter over the crispy breadcrumbs and torn basil leaves, then serve.

Photograph overleaf >

BUTTER CHICKEN CURRY

The perfect alternative to ordering from your local curry house. This can be quite rich, so I like to serve it with a cucumber salad or something similarly refreshing. For an all-out fake-away, you can serve it with rice and naan bread.

2 tablespoons salted butter

500 g (1 lb 2oz) chicken breast fillets, or 8 skinless, boneless chicken thighs, cut into strips

4 spring onions, sliced

1 garlic clove, grated

thumb-sized piece of fresh root ginger, grated

2 teaspoons garam masala

2 teaspoons ground coriander

2 teaspoons ground cumin

2 teaspoons ground turmeric

1 tablespoon tomato puree

400 ml can (14 fl oz) passata (sieved tomatoes)

200 ml (7 fl oz) double cream, plus a little extra to serve

sea salt and freshly ground black pepper

To serve

1 green chilli, sliced

freshly chopped coriander

2 limes, halved

cooked rice or naan bread (optional)

1 > Melt 1 tablespoon of the butter in a large saucepan over a medium–high heat. Add the chicken and fry for 3–4 minutes, until it's beginning to turn a little golden. Add the spring onions, garlic and ginger, along with a pinch of salt, and fry for 1 minute. Add the spices and cook for 1 minute more, then stir in the tomato puree and fry for a further 2 minutes. Pour the passata into the pan, reduce the heat to low and let it bubble away for 10–15 minutes.

2 > Now add the cream and the remaining butter, and season with salt and pepper to taste. Leave to simmer for a couple more minutes, until everything is warmed through, then remove from the heat and drizzle with a little more cream. Scatter over the green chilli and fresh coriander, and serve with the lime halves and rice or naan bread, if using.

6
SLOWER FOOD AND COMFORT COOKING

SLOW-COOKED LAMB AND CHICKPEA STEW

The five-hour cooking time sounds long, but once it's in the pot, you can leave this stew to simmer until you're ready to enjoy meltingly tender lamb.

1 tablespoon olive oil

1.2 kg–1.4 kg (2 lb 10 oz–3 lb 1 oz) lamb shoulder, bone in, or 800 g (1lb 12 oz) diced lamb shoulder

2 red onions, finely sliced

2 garlic cloves, finely sliced

2 tablespoons harissa paste

125 ml (4 fl oz) white wine

1 stock cube (vegetable or chicken)

1 small butternut squash (around 600 g/1 lb 5 oz), halved, deseeded and chopped into 3 cm (1¼ inch) chunks, peel left on

2 x 400 g (14 oz) cans chickpeas

200 g (7 oz) spinach, cavolo nero or spring greens

juice of 1 lemon

sea salt and freshly ground black pepper

To serve

crumbled feta

freshly chopped flat-leaf parsley

1 > Heat the olive oil in the base of a deep saucepan over a high heat. Season the lamb shoulder, then add to the pan, fat-side down. Fry for 3–5 minutes, until a deep golden brown. Use a pair of tongs to remove it from the pan and set aside on a plate. If you're using diced lamb, simply brown the chunks in the same way, then set aside on a plate.

2 > Reduce the heat slightly and add the onions to the pan, along with a big pinch of salt. Fry for 5 minutes, until the onions are beginning to soften. Add the garlic, fry for 2 minutes further, then stir in the harissa paste. Pour in the wine and bubble for 5 minutes, until it has reduced a little, then crumble in the stock cube and add 1 litre (1¾ pints) water. Bring to the boil and whisk to make sure the stock cube has fully dissolved.

3 > Reduce the heat right down to low and return the lamb to the pan. Cover with a sheet of tin foil, then top with the saucepan lid. Leave to simmer for 3½–4 hours, until the lamb is falling from the bone. Make sure the heat is low: you don't want to boil the lamb.

4 > If you are using a bone-in lamb shoulder, you should now be able to remove the bones easily. Take the pan off the heat and pull the bones out: the meat should slide off and remain in the pan. Discard the bones. Use a fork to gently pull the lamb into chunks, removing any fatty bits. Use a spoon to skim off any fat that has risen to the surface.

5 > Add the squash to the pan and return to the stove top over a medium heat. Cover with the saucepan lid and cook for a further 45 minutes.

6 > Now add the chickpeas, including the liquid from their cans. Increase the heat to medium–high and cook for 10 minutes, until the sauce thickens.

7 > Stir through the spinach, cavolo nero or greens and add half the lemon juice. Taste and season. Ladle the stew into 4 bowls and serve, topped with crumbled feta and chopped parsley.

MY ULTIMATE RATATOUILLE
WITH SOURDOUGH CROUTONS

This took me the longest time to perfect. For such a simple dish, there sure are a lot of different ways to make it! This is my favourite: it's a little sweet, a little sharp and a lotta comfort. Sometimes I make a double or even triple batch of the ratatouille as it's so versatile: toss it into pasta, pile it on top of toast or pizza, or just eat it straight out of the refrigerator when you need a snack. You can serve it with chunky bread rather than making the croutons, if you like, but in my eyes they take this dish from 'tasty dinner' to 'Wow! I want to eat this every night and tell all my friends about it!'

250 g (9 oz) sourdough bread, torn roughly into chunky cubes

3 tablespoons olive oil, plus extra for drizzling

2 small aubergines, cut into 3 cm (1¼ inch) chunks

2 small courgettes, halved lengthways and cut into rough chunks

2 red onions, cut into wedges

6 juicy and ripe tomatoes, around 400 g (14 oz), cut into wedges

2 garlic cloves, finely sliced

2 roasted red peppers from a jar, torn

400 g (14 oz) can tomatoes (either cherry or plum tomatoes – get the best quality you can, as it'll make a real difference here)

1 teaspoon caster or light brown sugar

1 > Place the chunks of bread in a large non-stick frying pan, off the heat. Drizzle over 2 tablespoons olive oil and season with salt and pepper, then use your hands to make sure the bread chunks are well coated in the oil. Now place the pan over a medium–high heat and fry for 6–8 minutes, tossing regularly, until you have crisp croutons that are charred in places. Transfer the croutons to a plate and set aside. Remove any crumbs from the pan.

2 > Keeping the pan over the same heat, add the aubergines and courgettes, along with a big pinch of salt, and dry-fry for around 8 minutes, tossing regularly, until charred and collapsing.

3 > Add 1 tablespoon olive oil to the pan, then toss in the red onion wedges with another pinch of salt. Give everything a good stir. Don't worry if your pan looks a little overcrowded; it'll all cook down. Fry for another 10 minutes, tossing regularly, until everything is softening and caramelizing.

1–2 tablespoons balsamic
     vinegar
sea salt and freshly ground black
     pepper
fresh basil leaves, to serve

4 > Now add the tomato wedges and garlic. Cook for a few minutes, then stir in the roasted red peppers. Stir to combine, then add the can of tomatoes, along with the sugar. Use the back of your spoon to smush the tomatoes into the mixture. Reduce the heat to low, cover with a lid and cook for 25 minutes.

5 > Remove the lid, increase the heat a little and simmer for 5 more minutes, stirring, so that the sauce reduces. Remove from the heat and stir in 1 tablespoon balsamic vinegar. Taste and add another tablespoon if you feel it needs it: it will depend on how acidic your tomatoes are. Season to taste.

6 > Scatter the crispy croutons on top, pressing them into the mixture slightly. Rest for a few minutes, then top with basil and drizzle over a little olive oil. Finish with a crack of black pepper and serve.

Photograph overleaf >

SPANISH CHICKEN AND CHORIZO STEW

This dish could be a weekend wonder or a midweek classic – the chorizo gives it just the right level of spice and smokiness and the whole dish leaves you feeling a little indulged and super satisfied. It's perfect for feeding a crowd – serve it with a big salad.

1 teaspoon olive oil

2 red onions, cut into wedges

2 red peppers, cored, deseeded
    and cut into 1 cm (½ inch) slices

200 g (7 oz) ring chorizo, peeled
    and cut into 5mm (¼ inch)
    slices

6 skinless, boneless chicken
    thighs, each cut into 3 or 4
    pieces, about 450 g (1 lb)
    in total

2 cloves garlic, grated

1 teaspoon sweet smoked
    paprika

1 tablespoon tomato puree

125 ml (4 fl oz) white wine

2 x 400 g (14 oz) cans cannellini
    beans, drained but not rinsed

1 chicken stock cube

small bunch of fresh flat-leaf
    parsley, roughly chopped

100 g (3½ oz) green olives, halved

sea salt

lemon wedges, to serve

1 > Heat the olive oil in a large non-stick, high-sided frying pan over a medium–high heat. Add the red onion wedges and red peppers, along with a pinch of salt, and fry for around 5 minutes, stirring regularly. Add the chorizo slices and the chicken and fry for 5 minutes further. Add the garlic and fry for 2 minutes more, then add the smoked paprika and tomato puree and stir well so that everything is coated.

2 > Pour the wine into the pan and simmer until the liquid is reduced by half. Add the cannellini beans. Half-fill one of the emptied cans with water and pour that into the pan too. Add the stock cube and bring to the boil, stirring to make sure the stock cube has dissolved. Stir in most of the parsley.

3 > Reduce the heat to medium–low and bubble away for 8–10 minutes more, until the sauce has reduced and the chicken is cooked through.

4 > Scatter over the green olives and remaining parsley, and serve with lemon wedges.

MACKEREL WITH FRIED POTATOES

AND SALSA VERDE

Salsa verde is the kind of sauce you make once and then insist on pairing with nearly everything you cook. Make extra and stir it through yogurt to make the world's best dip. Serve this dish with a fresh tomato salad and transport yourself to a beachside restaurant in the Mediterranean. If you don't have a mini chopper, you can chop the ingredients for the salsa verde by hand and combine them in a bowl.

1 generous tablespoon olive oil

800 g (1 lb 12 oz) potatoes, peeled and chopped into 2 cm (¾ inch) chunks

4 smoked mackerel fillets (I like to use peppered fillets), about 140 g (5 oz) each

sea salt and freshly ground black pepper

For the salsa verde

3 large handfuls of fresh herbs (I use a mix of parsley, dill and tarragon)

4 tablespoons capers

50 g (1¾ oz) can anchovies (optional)

juice of 1 lemon

1 garlic clove

pinch of caster sugar

3–4 tablespoons olive oil

To serve

handful of watercress

lemon wedges

1 > Heat the olive oil in a large non-stick frying pan over a medium–high heat. When it's very hot, add the chopped potatoes, along with a big pinch of salt. Reduce the heat to medium and fry for 10–15 minutes, stirring regularly, until the potatoes are a deep golden colour, crisp and cooked through. Check them for doneness with a knife: it should slide through.

2 > While the potatoes are frying, make the salsa verde. Simply put all the ingredients (except the olive oil) in a mini chopper. If you're using the anchovies, you can include the oil from their can. Pulse into a roughly chopped paste, then pour over the olive oil to make it a drizzle-able consistency. Season well with salt and pepper and set aside until needed.

3 > Add the mackerel fillets to the frying pan, breaking them up as you go. Toss gently, to combine with the potatoes and heat the fish through. Take the pan off the heat, allow to cool a little, then drizzle with some of the salsa verde.

4 > Serve with a handful of watercress and lemon wedges, plus any remaining salsa verde.

MARMITE AND FRENCH ONION SOUP

This is Friday-night-in food. The sweet, slow-cooked onions complement the tang of the Marmite perfectly. It's also topped with a big crispy chunk of bread and grated cheese (in case you were thinking that soup can't be an indulgent dinner). Swap the beef stock for veggie if you want a meat-free meal. The booze option is up to you: I usually just go with what I have in the house. Beer will give a heavier flavour, whereas wine or cider will make it a little lighter. The choice is yours!

2 tablespoons salted butter

2 thick slices of bread (I like sourdough or ciabatta)

50 g (1¾ oz) Gruyère cheese, finely grated

1 tablespoon olive oil

600 g (1 lb 5 oz) onions, finely sliced

1 garlic clove, sliced

1 teaspoon caster sugar

2 teaspoons self-raising flour

75 ml (2½ fl oz) cider, beer or white wine

500 ml (18 fl oz) beef stock

1 tablespoon Marmite (or Bovril)

1 tablespoon balsamic vinegar

sea salt

1 > Melt half a tablespoon of the butter in a large saucepan over a medium–high heat. Once melted and foaming, add the bread slices and fry on each side until golden. Transfer the slices to a chopping board and immediately scatter over half the grated cheese. Set aside, but don't cover, or they will go soggy.

2 > Reduce the heat to medium. Add the remaining butter to the saucepan, along with the olive oil. Tip the onions into the pan with a big pinch of salt. Cook for 15–20 minutes, stirring regularly, until softened and turning golden. Don't rush this: it's the key to the flavour! If the onions start to catch on the base of the pan, add a splash of water.

3 > Add the garlic and sugar and cook for 3 minutes further, stirring constantly. Now add the flour and stir to coat all the onion mixture. Cook for 1 minute: this cooks away the raw flour taste. Pour in the cider, beer or wine and whisk as it quickly absorbs. Add the stock slowly, whisking as you pour it in. Cover with a lid and cook for 10 minutes, then add the Marmite and balsamic vinegar and season to taste.

4 > Divide the soup between 2 bowls. Top each one with a slice of cheesy bread and finish with a layer of the remaining grated Gruyère.

BEEF, ALE AND MIXED GRAIN STEW
WITH SPICY YOGURT

I initially wrote this recipe without the yogurt, but when I first tested it, I felt like something was missing. Enter the spicy yogurt, which manages to be cooling at the same time as bringing the heat. It's worth making extra to spoon on to everything else you eat this week!

2 tablespoons olive oil
500 g (1 lb 2 oz) stewing beef, cut into 3 cm (1¼ inch) chunks
400 g (14 oz) carrots, cut into 3 cm (1¼ inch) chunks
3 celery sticks, cut into 3 cm (1¼ inch) chunks
2 onions, cut into wedges
½ tablespoon plain flour
350 ml (12 fl oz) ale or beer
2 bay leaves
2 garlic cloves
750 ml (1⅓ pints) beef stock
2 x 250 g (9 oz) pouches ready-cooked mixed grains (or a mixture of cooked grains such as rice and lentils)
2 teaspoons red wine vinegar
sea salt and freshly ground black pepper

For the spicy yogurt
1 teaspoon dried chilli flakes
150 ml (5 fl oz) Greek yogurt
1 teaspoon red wine vinegar

1 > Heat 1 tablespoon olive oil in a large non-stick saucepan over a high heat. Season the beef chunks and add them to the pan in an even layer. Let them fry for 3–5 minutes, until browned. They will initially stick to the base of the pan, but once brown, they will release. Turn over the beef chunks and brown on the other side for 3 minutes. Tip on to a plate and set aside.

2 > Add the remaining oil to the pan and add the carrots, celery and onions. Cook for around 5 minutes, stirring occasionally, until starting to char in places. Add the flour and stir to make a sandy mixture. Pour in the ale or beer and add the bay leaves. Leaving the skin on the garlic cloves, bash them with the side of a knife and add them to the pan. Pour in the beef stock, bring to the boil, then reduce the heat to very low.

3 > Return the beef to the pan and stir. Cover with a sheet of tin foil, then top with the saucepan lid to hold the tin foil down. Cook for 3½ hours, until the chunks of beef are meltingly tender.

4 > Meanwhile, make the spicy yogurt. In a small bowl, mix together the chilli flakes, yogurt and red wine vinegar. Season well and set aside in the refrigerator until needed.

5 > Once the beef is cooked, stir in the ready-cooked mixed grains. Bring the stew back to the boil and cook for 2–3 minutes, until it thickens a little. Stir in the red wine vinegar and season with salt and pepper. Spoon into 4 bowls and serve with the spicy yogurt.

WINTER ROOTS TAGINE

The perfect dish for those days when you want to go meat-free, this tagine is just as satisfying as its meaty alternative, but it packs in a host of your daily vegetables. Be generous with the tahini drizzle, you won't regret it.

1 tablespoon olive oil

1 red onion, finely sliced

500 g (1 lb 2 oz) carrots, quartered lengthways and cut into 5 cm (2 inch) lengths

500 g (1 lb 2 oz) parsnips, quartered lengthways and cut into 5 cm (2 inch) lengths

1 garlic clove, finely sliced

2 teaspoons ground cinnamon

2 teaspoons ground cumin

2 teaspoons paprika

1 tablespoon tomato puree

2 vegetable stock cubes

5 Medjool dates, stoned and roughly chopped

2 x 400 g (14 oz) cans chickpeas

handful of fresh mint, leaves and stalks separated

200 g (7 oz) couscous

juice of 1 lemon

sea salt and freshly ground black pepper

For the pickled onions

1 red onion, finely sliced

juice of 1 lemon

To serve

tahini

toasted flaked almonds

1 > Begin by preparing the pickled onions. Place the red onion slices in a bowl and pour over the lemon juice. Add a big pinch of salt and scrunch the onions with your hands to soften. Set aside to pickle while you make the tagine.

2 > Heat the olive oil in a large saucepan over a medium–high heat. Add the onion, along with a big pinch of salt, followed by the carrots and parsnips. Fry for 10 minutes, stirring regularly.

3 > Add the garlic to the pan and fry for 1 minute, then add the spices. Stir so the spices coat all the veg and let them cook for 1 minute: this will stop the tagine tasting of raw spice. Now stir in the tomato puree, followed by 750 ml (1⅓ pints) water. Crumble in the stock cubes, bring to the boil and stir to make sure the stock cubes have dissolved.

4 > Add the dates and reduce the heat to low. Add the chickpeas, along with the liquid from their cans, and a handful of the mint stalks. Simmer for 15 minutes, until the carrots and parsnips are nearly softened.

5 > Meanwhile, place the couscous in a large bowl, add a big pinch of salt and pour over 200 ml (7 fl oz) boiling water. Cover with clingfilm and set aside.

6 > Once the carrots and parsnips have softened, increase the heat and simmer for 5–10 minutes until the sauce has reduced to a slightly thicker, glossier consistency. Scoop out the mint stalks, then stir in the lemon juice and season well.

7 > Remove the clingfilm from the couscous and use a fork to fluff it up. Spoon the couscous into 4 bowls and top with the tagine. Drizzle each serving with tahini, then scatter over the flaked almonds and mint leaves, and top with the pickled onions.

PAELLA SMASHED POTATOES

*Paella is amazing and I'm not here to cast any doubt on that: swapping the rice
for potatoes here is really more of an ode to the original. That said, the crispy
potatoes dosed in chorizo oil really do give the rice a run for its money.
I'm sold!*

400 g (14 oz) potatoes, peeled
and cut into 2 cm (¾ inch)
cubes
1 tablespoon + 1 teaspoon olive
oil
1 red onion, sliced
1 red pepper, cored, deseeded
and sliced
100 g (3½ oz) chorizo, cut into
slices 5 mm (⅛ inch) thick
1 garlic clove, grated
1 teaspoon smoked paprika
180 g (6½ oz) raw king prawns
100 g (3½ oz) frozen peas
juice of ½ lemon
handful of fresh flat-leaf parsley,
roughly chopped
sea salt and freshly ground black
pepper

1 > Heat 180 ml (6½ fl oz) water in a non-stick frying pan over a medium–
high heat. Add the potatoes with a big pinch of salt and 1 teaspoon
olive oil. Cover with a lid and cook for 10–12 minutes, shaking the pan
regularly so the potatoes don't stick.

2 > Remove the lid. Add 1 tablespoon olive oil to the pan, then stir in the
red onion, red pepper and chorizo. Fry for around 10 minutes, until the
potatoes are soft. Smush the potatoes a bit with a spatula so they
can fry a little in the chorizo-flavoured oil.

3 > Add the garlic and smoked paprika and stir well to combine, breaking
up the potatoes as you do so. Add the prawns and frozen peas and
toss everything together well to heat through.

4 > Squeeze in a little lemon juice, then taste and season. Scatter with
parsley and serve with the remaining lemon juice to taste.

HAM, POTATO AND KALE STEW
WITH CRÈME FRAÎCHE

This is all about the quality of your ingredients. Use the chunkiest ham hock you can find; if you can get your hands on some from the butcher that you can shred into chunks yourself, you're in for a real treat!

1 tablespoon olive oil
1 large onion, finely sliced
1 garlic clove, sliced
125 ml (4 fl oz) white wine
1 litre (1¾ pints) chicken stock
2 bay leaves
500 g (1 lb 2 oz) baby potatoes, larger ones halved and small ones left whole
1 teaspoon English mustard
300 g (10½ oz) pre-cooked ham hock (or you can use chunks of ham or gammon), chopped into pieces
150 g (5 ½ oz) kale, torn and tough stems removed
200 g (7 oz) frozen peas
juice of ½ lemon, plus extra to taste
sea salt and freshly ground black pepper

To serve
crème fraîche
fresh mint leaves
garlic bread

1 > Heat the olive oil in a large saucepan over a medium heat. Add the onion, along with a large pinch of salt, and fry for about 5 minutes, until softened.

2 > Add the garlic and fry for 2 minutes, then pour in the wine and bubble until reduced by half. Add the stock and bay leaves, along with the potatoes, and turn up the heat. Bring to the boil and cook for 15–20 minutes or until the potatoes are soft.

3 > Once the potatoes are cooked, add the mustard, cooked ham, kale and frozen peas and cook for 2–3 minutes, until everything is heated through and the peas are bright green. Squeeze in the lemon juice, taste and season. Add a little more lemon juice if you wish.

4 > Ladle the stew into 4 bowls and top each one with a dollop of crème fraîche and a scattering of fresh mint. Serve with garlic bread.

Photograph overleaf >

SAUSAGE CASSOULET

This is hearty, but it's also refined. It's the kind of dish you might enjoy at a restaurant without realizing how easily you could recreate it at home.

1 tablespoon olive oil
8 pork sausages or chipolatas, such as Cumberland
2 onions, finely sliced
4 sprigs each of fresh rosemary and thyme
2 garlic cloves, finely sliced
1 teaspoon fennel seeds
1 teaspoon dried chilli flakes
2 x 400 g (14 oz) cans white haricot, cannellini or butter beans, drained but not rinsed
1 stock cube (beef, vegetable or chicken)
200 g (7 oz) spring greens, sliced
1 tablespoon wholegrain mustard
1 lemon
sea salt and freshly ground black pepper
handful of fresh flat-leaf parsley, to serve

1 > Heat the olive oil in a large saucepan over a medium–high heat. Add the sausages and fry for around 8 minutes until browned, shaking the pan so they colour evenly. Set the sausages aside on a plate.

2 > Add the onions to the pan, along with a big pinch of salt. Fry for 10 minutes, until soft and a little golden. You can add a splash of water if the onion starts to stick at all.

3 > Add the rosemary and thyme, along with the garlic, fennel seeds and chilli flakes. Stir well and cook for 2 minutes, until the garlic has started to turn golden. Tip in the beans. Refill one of the emptied cans with water and pour that into the pan too. Bring to the boil and crumble in the stock cube. Stir to combine, then reduce the heat to low. Return the sausages to the pan and cook for 10 minutes, until the sauce has the consistency of a thin gravy.

4 > Remove the rosemary and thyme stalks from the pan and discard. Stir in the spring greens along with the mustard, then squeeze in the juice of half the lemon and season well. Cook for 1 minute further, so the greens are cooked through, then spoon into 4 bowls and top with the parsley. Serve with the other half of the lemon on the table, in case anyone wants a squeeze more.

7
FANCIER FOOD

LAMB LEG AND GIANT COUSCOUS
WITH MINTY YOGURT

If you want to show off to a group of friends, this is a bit of showstopper.
You can leave the lamb to rest for up to 30 minutes before serving if you like.

1 tablespoon olive oil

600 g (1 lb 5 oz) boneless leg of
   lamb, cut into 4 large chunks

1 red onion, finely sliced

3 celery sticks, finely sliced

1 tablespoon ras el hanout

50 g (1¾ oz) dried apricots,
   roughly chopped

50 g (1¾ oz) sultanas or raisins

350 g (12 oz) giant couscous

1 litre (1¾ pints) chicken stock

1 tablespoon red wine vinegar

large bunch of fresh flat-leaf
   parsley, chopped

3 tablespoons toasted pine nuts

sea salt and freshly ground black
   pepper

For the minty yogurt

200 ml (7 fl oz) Greek yogurt

2 tablespoons store-bought mint
   sauce

1 > First make the minty yogurt. Mix together the yogurt and mint sauce in a small bowl with a big pinch of salt and pepper. Set aside.

2 > Heat 1 tablespoon olive oil in a large high-sided, non-stick frying pan over a high heat. While the pan is heating up, place the lamb in a large bowl and add 3 tablespoons of the minty yogurt. Toss until the lamb is well coated in the sauce. Once the pan is very hot, add the lamb pieces and fry for around 2½ minutes on each side until golden.

3 > Reduce the heat to medium–low and add a big splash of water to release some of the char from the base of the pan. Cover with a lid and cook the lamb for 10 more minutes (this will give you medium-rare meat). If your lamb chunks vary in size, adjust the cooking time and remove the smaller pieces a little earlier to avoid overcooking them.

4 > Lay out a large sheet of tin foil on the kitchen surface. Using a pair of tongs, transfer the lamb on to the tin foil and wrap it up to rest. If the pan is extremely charred, give it a quick wipe before returning it to the heat.

5 > Add the onion and celery to the frying pan, along with a big pinch of salt, and fry for 5–7 minutes, until soft. Add the ras el hanout, apricots, sultanas or raisins and giant couscous and stir well. Pour in the stock and bring to the boil. Cook according to the couscous packet instructions (usually around 10 minutes), until the couscous is tender with a slight bite.

6 > Stir in the red wine vinegar and most of the parsley and season to taste. Slice the rested lamb pieces, and tip any lamb juices into the couscous. To serve, divide the couscous between 4 plates and top with the sliced lamb and the remaining mint yogurt. Scatter over the toasted pine nuts and reserved parsley.

SEAFOOD AND SWEETCORN CHOWDER

On the surface, this chowder is pretty simple. However, cooking the eggs in the pan, then fishing them out to peel, is a stroke of genius, saving on washing-up. I love the green chilli, but feel free to leave it out if you don't like a little spice.

1 tablespoon olive oil

1 onion, finely sliced

2 leeks, trimmed, cleaned and finely sliced

½ green chilli, deseeded and finely chopped (optional)

small bunch of fresh coriander, stems finely chopped, leaves separated

500 g (1 lb 2 oz) baby potatoes, halved (larger ones can be quartered)

500 ml (18 fl oz) fish stock

4 eggs

200 ml (7 fl oz) milk

250 g (9 oz) smoked haddock fillets

2 x 200 g (7 oz) cans sweetcorn

360 g (12½ oz) raw king prawns

sea salt and freshly ground black pepper

1 > Heat the olive oil in a large saucepan over a medium–high heat. Add the onion, leeks, green chilli and coriander stems to the pan, along with a big pinch of salt. Fry for around 3 minutes until soft, stirring regularly.

2 > Add the potatoes to the pan, along with the fish stock and 100 ml (3½ fl oz) water. Bring to the boil and add the eggs, whole and in their shells. Boil for 6 minutes.

3 > Using a slotted spoon, carefully remove the eggs and set them aside in a bowl. Add the milk to the pan, then reduce the heat right down to low. Add the smoked haddock, cover with a lid and simmer for 8 minutes further, until the haddock is flaking apart.

4 > Meanwhile, rinse the eggs with cold water and peel.

5 > Add the sweetcorn and prawns to the pan. Stir well and cook for 2 minutes further, until the prawns are bright pink. Season and spoon the chowder into 4 bowls. Halve the eggs and serve each bowlful of chowder topped with 2 egg halves and a scattering of coriander leaves.

DATE NIGHT RAGU

This dish gets its name because a friend of mine likes to make it when he first cooks for potential love interests. He would argue that love is much more likely to blossom over this pasta than any other dish. Disclaimer: I know this recipe makes more than two servings. That still makes it an ideal date night meal, though, because if the date goes terribly, you can at least console yourself with thoughts of leftover ragu to enjoy in the days to follow.

500 g (1 lb 2 oz) stewing steak (use a cut like shin or cheeks), cut into chunks
2 tablespoons olive oil
1 red onion, roughly chopped
2 garlic cloves, grated
1 tablespoon tomato puree
200 ml (7 fl oz) red wine
400 g (14 oz) can chopped tomatoes
1 beef stock cube
sprigs of rosemary and thyme and a bay leaf (all or any that you have)
1 tablespoon Marmite or soy sauce
400 g (14 oz) dried pappardelle or tagliatelle (halve this if you're cooking for two)
sea salt and freshly ground black pepper

To serve
shavings of Parmesan cheese
basil leaves

1 > Season the beef with salt and pepper. Heat 1 tablespoon olive oil in a large saucepan over a high heat. Add the beef and let it sit for 2–3 minutes, until the pieces release when you wiggle them with a pair of tongs: they should be well coloured. Turn them over and repeat the browning on the other side. Remove the beef from the pan and set aside on a plate.

2 > Reduce the heat to medium and add the remaining olive oil, then the onion, along with a big pinch of salt. Use your spatula or spoon to scrape the base of the pan and mix any of the released meaty goodness into the onion. Cook for around 5 minutes until softened. Add the garlic and cook for 2 minutes longer.

3 > Add the tomato puree and stir so it cooks a little, then pour in the red wine. Let it bubble away until the liquid is reduced by half, giving the base of the pan another little scrape as it bubbles, then tip in the can of tomatoes. Refill the emptied can with water twice and pour that into the pan too, along with the beef stock cube. Bring to the boil, stirring well to make sure the stock cube has dissolved, then reduce the heat to a simmer.

4 > Return the beef to the pan, add the herbs and cover with a sheet of foil, followed by the lid. Cook for 3 hours, until the beef falls apart when gently prodded. If it's not quite there, return the lid and cook for 30 minutes further.

Continued overleaf >

5 > Remove the herb stalks from the sauce and use two forks to shred the beef in the pan. (You can use a slotted spoon to remove the beef and shred it on a plate, then return it to the pan, if that's easier for you.) Stir in the Marmite or soy sauce, taste and season. The sauce will be quite watery, but don't worry, the pasta will soak it all up. If you're cooking for two, remove half the sauce from the pan and set it aside to cool.

6 > Increase the heat to medium–high. Once the sauce is bubbling away, add the pasta. Stir well, then cover with a lid and cook for 10–12 minutes, stirring regularly and adding a splash of water if it starts to look dry. Test the pasta for doneness: if it's still a little firm, add a big splash of water and continue to cook, stirring, until the pasta is cooked and the sauce is coating the pasta. If the sauce needs loosening, simply add a splash more water.

7 > Twirl into bowls and serve, topped with Parmesan shavings and some basil leaves.

Tip >
Leftover sauce will keep in the refrigerator in an airtight container for 3–5 days. When ready to serve it again, make sure to bring the sauce to the boil before adding the pasta, then continue with step 6. You may need to add a little more water.

MASALA MUSSELS

There's no denying that this dish is messy: you can't eat it without using your hands to pick the meat from the mussels and mop up all that lovely sauce with naan bread. Once everything is prepped, it's a really speedy meal, so make sure you're ready to eat before you chuck the mussels in the pan.

1 kg (2 lb 4 oz) mussels, cleaned (see step 1)
1 tablespoon olive oil
small bunch of spring onions, sliced
1 garlic clove, grated
thumb-sized piece of fresh root ginger, grated
1 tablespoon tomato puree
70 g (2½ oz) masala curry paste
300 ml (10 fl oz) double cream
1 lime, ½ juiced and ½ cut into wedges
small bunch of fresh coriander, roughly chopped
sea salt and freshly ground black pepper
naan bread, to serve

1 > Make sure your mussels are clean and prepped, removing any beards and scrubbing them well in cold running water. Discard any mussels that stay open when you tap them. Set the mussels to one side in a large bowl covered with a tea towel.

2 > Heat the olive oil in the base of a deep saucepan over a medium–high heat. Add the spring onions, garlic and ginger along with a big pinch of salt. Fry for 2 minutes, then stir in the tomato puree. Add the curry paste and stir well to combine. Cook for a couple of minutes, then pour in the double cream. Fill the cream pot with water and add that to the pan too. Season well.

3 > Cook for around 5 minutes, then add the lime juice. Tip in the mussels and cover with a lid. Cook on a high heat for 3 minutes, until the shells have opened (discard any that remain closed). Spoon the mussels into bowls and top with the coriander. Serve immediately, with the lime wedges for squeezing over and the naan bread on the side.

Photograph overleaf >

BROWN BUTTER GNOCCHI
WITH CRISPY SAGE

If you want to create a restaurant-style dish in 15 minutes, this gnocchi number is the one for you. Be sure to serve it with a sharp green salad – this is a crucial element.

handful of fresh sage leaves
2 tablespoons salted butter
1 tablespoon olive oil
350 g (12 oz) gnocchi
25 g (1 oz) Parmesan cheese,
   finely grated
zest of 1 unwaxed lemon
sea salt and freshly ground black
   pepper
green salad, to serve
   (not optional!)

1 > Start by making the crispy sage. Melt the butter in a large non-stick frying pan over a medium heat and cook for around 3 minutes, whisking constantly. The butter will turn foamy, then begin to brown and smell nutty: I always think it smells a bit like digestive biscuits! Add the sage leaves and fry for about 1 minute, until they go dark green. Remove the pan from the heat and scoop out the sage leaves using a slotted spoon. Set them aside on a plate lined with kitchen roll.

2 > Put the pan back on the heat and add the olive oil: this will stop the butter from getting too brown and burning. Add the gnocchi to the pan and fry for 2–3 minutes, tossing regularly, until they're a little golden on either side. Add 100 ml (3½ fl oz) boiling water to the pan and cover with a lid. Cook for 2 minutes.

3 > Remove the lid and toss well so the butter and water combine to make a silky sauce. Add most of the grated Parmesan, tossing the pan constantly as you do so: this will help the Parmesan melt into the sauce. Don't worry if the sauce splits. Just add a splash more water and keep tossing over a high heat: it will come back together. Season well, then tip into 2 bowls. Top with the crispy sage and the remaining Parmesan. Zest the lemon over the top (you can use the lemon juice for the salad dressing) and finish with a crack of black pepper. Serve with a sharp green salad.

STEAK, LENTILS AND BEETROOT
WITH HORSERADISH YOGURT

There are a few key tricks to cooking steak. Firstly, begin by frying or 'rendering' the fatty edges. This makes the fat delicious and crisp rather than chewy. Second, use a timer. Third, baste, baste, baste! Spooning the butter over the steak as it cooks makes it so darn tasty. Finally, rest the meat. Allow the steak to sit while the lentils are cooking, to reabsorb all the delicious juices.

2 sirloin steaks, around 225 g (8 oz) each

1 tablespoon olive oil

2 tablespoons salted butter

1 red onion, finely sliced

250 g (9 oz) pre-cooked beetroots, drained and chopped into 2 cm (¾ inch) chunks

1 garlic clove, grated

75 ml (2½ fl oz) red wine

250 g (9 oz) pouch pre-cooked puy lentils

1 tablespoon horseradish sauce

2 tablespoons Greek yogurt

juice of 1 lemon

½ small bunch of fresh flat-leaf parsley, roughly chopped

sea salt and freshly ground black pepper

1 > Heat a large non-stick frying pan over a high heat. Rub the steaks with the olive oil. Once the pan is really hot, use tongs to hold the steaks on their sides so just the strip of fat is touching the hot pan. Hold like this for around 1 minute, until the fat is turning golden and crisping up, then place the steaks flat in the pan. Cook for 1½ minutes (for rare) or 2 minutes (medium-rare). Flip the steaks over and add the butter to the pan. As the butter melts, tip the pan away from you and use a tablespoon to keep spooning the melted butter and juices over the steaks. Cook in this way for 1½ minutes or 2 minutes, as before, then remove the pan from the heat. Set the steaks aside on a plate. Season them with salt and pepper, cover with foil, and leave to rest.

2> Return the pan to a medium–high heat. Add the onion along with a pinch of salt. Fry for 5 minutes, until softening, then add the beetroot chunks and cook for 2 minutes more. Add the garlic and toss well. Pour in the red wine and simmer for 2 minutes, then tip in the lentils. Reduce the heat to low, season and cook for 5 minutes.

3 > Meanwhile, in a small bowl, mix together the horseradish and the Greek yogurt. Add a dash of lemon juice and season well.

4 > Slice the steaks, tipping any juice from the plate or chopping board into the pan of lentils.

5 > Stir the remaining lemon juice into the lentils, then stir in most of the parsley. Spoon the lentils on to 2 plates and top with a dollop of the horseradish yogurt and the sliced beef. Scatter with the remaining parsley and finish with a crack of black pepper.

FISH STEW

This is one of my favourite recipes in the book: it's impressive, speedy and a great one to whip up when you want to show off a bit. A rouille is basically posh mayonnaise. I make a cheat's version here to serve on top.

500 g (1 lb 2 oz) mussels
1 tablespoon olive oil
1 onion, thickly sliced
3 celery sticks, chopped into 3 cm
  (1¼ inch) lengths
1 garlic clove, finely sliced
1 teaspoon fennel seeds
50 g (1¾ oz) can anchovies
400 g (14 oz) baby potatoes,
  halved
250 ml (9 fl oz) white wine
500 ml (18 fl oz) passata
700 ml (1¼ pints) fish stock
500 g (1 lb 2 oz) fish (I use a mix
  of salmon and cod, but any
  chunky white fish works well),
  cut into large chunks
180 g (6½ oz) raw peeled king
  prawns
juice of ½ lemon
sea salt and freshly ground black
  pepper
bunch of fresh flat-leaf parsley,
  roughly chopped, to serve
salad and chunky garlic bread,
  to serve

For the 'rouille'
2 tablespoons mayonnaise
2 tablespoons Greek yogurt
1 garlic clove, grated
juice of ½ lemon

1 > Make sure your mussels are clean and prepped, scrubbing them well in cold running water and removing any beards. Discard any mussels that stay open when you tap them. Set the prepped mussels to one side in a large bowl covered with a tea towel.

2 > Heat the olive oil in a large saucepan over a medium–high heat. Add the onion and celery, along with a pinch of salt, and fry for around 10 minutes, until softened.

3> Add the garlic and fennel seeds and stir, then tip the whole can of anchovies into the pan, including their oil. Fry for a couple of minutes until the anchovies have practically 'melted' into the veg. Add the potatoes and stir, then add the white wine and let it bubble for a couple of minutes.

4 > Pour the passata and fish stock into the pan. Bring to the boil, then reduce the heat a little, cover with a lid and cook for 20 minutes. Remove the lid and cook for 10 minutes further, until the potatoes are cooked through (check them with a knife: it should slide straight through).

5 > Meanwhile, in a small bowl mix together the ingredients for the cheat's rouille. Season well and set aside.

6 > Add the fish, prawns and mussels to the pan. Cover with a lid and cook for 5 minutes until the prawns have turned bright pink and the mussels have fully opened (discard any that remain closed). Remove from the heat and stir in the lemon juice, then taste and season.

7 > Spoon the stew into 4 bowls, and top each serving with a spoonful of rouille and a few parsley leaves. Add a crack of black pepper. This is best served with a salad and some chunks of garlic bread.

DUCK AND CITRUS RICE

This dish plays on the senses, combining the age-old pairing of duck and orange with the fragrant spices used in Chinese duck dishes. It's a tantalizing blend of sweet, salty and spicy that ticks all the right boxes. If you can't get hold of duck, you can use chicken breasts with the skin on instead, but make sure the chicken is cooked all the way through – you don't want to serve it pink like the duck!

2 duck breasts, about 150 g (5¼ oz) each
4 spring onions, sliced
1 garlic clove
thumb-sized piece of fresh root ginger, grated
pinch of dried chilli flakes (optional)
2 star anise
1 teaspoon clear honey
250 g (9 oz) pouch ready-cooked basmati rice
zest and juice of 1 orange
1 tablespoon soy sauce
100 g (3½ oz) spinach
handful of freshly chopped coriander
sea salt and freshly ground black pepper

1 > Heat a large non-stick frying pan over a high heat. Season the fatty side of the duck breasts with a big pinch of salt. Once the pan is hot, add the duck breasts and cook for 6 minutes, until the fat is golden and crisp, pressing down on the duck breast with a fish slice to encourage the fat to cook. Flip the duck breasts over and cook on the other side for 4–5 minutes, then transfer the duck breasts to a plate or chopping board, leaving the juices in the pan. Cover the breasts with foil and set aside.

2 > Reduce the heat to medium–high, add the spring onions, garlic and ginger to the pan, along with a pinch of salt, and fry for 1 minute. Add the chilli flakes, if using, and the star anise. Toast for 2 minutes more, then add the honey and stir. Tip the rice into the pan, along with a splash of water. Use your spoon to break up the rice and mix everything together.

3 > Add the orange zest and half the juice, followed by the soy sauce. Stir to combine, then add the spinach, along with another splash of water. Stir well for about 2 minutes, until the spinach wilts down. Now stir through most of the coriander and season well.

4 > Slice the duck breasts, tipping any of the juice on the plate or chopping board into the rice pan. Spoon the rice into 2 bowls and top with the duck breast slices. Scatter over the reserved coriander leaves and serve with the remaining orange juice to taste.

CHICKEN AND PEANUT LETTUCE CUPS

If you're looking for a meal that's on the lighter side, but not 'so-light-I'm-left-unsatisfied' light, these lettuce cups are the go-to recipe. They're also really fun to eat, as you can sit around and build them as you would fajitas. I'd recommend serving them with ice-cold beers – and maybe some kitchen paper for cleaning sticky hands.

1 tablespoon sesame, vegetable or olive oil

6 skinless, boneless chicken thighs, each sliced into 4–5 strips, about 450 g (1 lb) in total

1½ tablespoons soy sauce

1½ tablespoons sriracha

1½ tablespoons peanut butter

juice of 1½ limes

175 g (6 oz) baby corn, halved lengthways

½ small bunch of spring onions, sliced

1 garlic clove, grated

thumb-sized piece of fresh root ginger, grated

sea salt and freshly ground black pepper

To serve

2 little gem lettuces, washed and pulled apart into big leaves

1 cucumber, sliced

large handful roasted, salted peanuts, roughly chopped

fresh coriander, roughly chopped

½ lime, cut into wedges

1 > Heat the oil in a large non-stick frying pan over a high heat. Add the chicken strips, along with a big pinch of salt. Fry for 8–10 minutes, tossing regularly, until the chicken is nice and golden.

2 > Meanwhile, in a small bowl or jug, whisk together the soy sauce, sriracha, peanut butter and lime juice, along with 1 tablespoon of water, to make a sauce. Season well.

3 > When the chicken is cooked, remove the pan from the heat and use two forks to very roughly shred the chicken. Return to the heat and add the baby corn and spring onions. Cook for 2–3 minutes, then add the garlic and ginger. Fry for another minute, then add the sauce. Toss well and season.

4 > Remove from the heat and serve straight from the pan, with the lettuce leaves, sliced cucumber, roasted peanuts, fresh coriander and lime wedges in serving dishes alongside. Let your guests build their own lettuce cups at the table.

Photograph overleaf >

CRAB AND ROSÉ SPAGHETTI

This sounds lavish – and it kinda is. However, it's also so simple and speedy that you might surprise yourself into making restaurant-quality food without trying all that hard! I use rosé wine because it's great to drink while you eat the pasta, but if you want to use white wine instead, go for it.

1 tablespoon olive oil

1 onion, finely sliced

1 garlic clove, finely sliced

pinch of dried chilli flakes

75 ml (2½ fl oz) rosé wine

150 g (5½ oz) cherry tomatoes

500 ml (18 fl oz) stock (fish or vegetable)

200 g (7 oz) dried spaghetti

100 g (3½ oz) crab meat (I use a 'half and half' mix of brown and white meat)

juice of 1 lemon

small bunch of fresh flat-leaf parsley or dill, roughly chopped

sea salt and freshly ground black pepper

1 > Heat the olive oil in a large saucepan over a medium heat. Add the onion, along with a big pinch of salt, and gently fry for 5 minutes, stirring regularly.

2 > Once the onion has softened, add the garlic and chilli flakes and fry for 2 minutes further. Add the rosé wine and bubble away for 5 minutes, until the liquid has reduced by around half. Tip in the cherry tomatoes, along with the stock. Season with salt and pepper and bring to the boil.

3 > Drop the pasta into the pan and use a pair of tongs to submerge it in the liquid. Cover the saucepan with a lid and cook for 10 minutes, until all the liquid has been absorbed and the pasta is cooked. Add a splash more water if all the stock has been absorbed but the pasta is still al dente.

4 > Stir the crab meat into the pasta, along with the lemon juice and most of the parsley or dill. Spoon the pasta into 2 bowls. Top with the remaining parsley or dill and a crack of black pepper, and serve.

8
SPEEDY SWEETS AND PARTY PUDDINGS

CHOCOLATE LAVA FRENCH TOAST

These little parcels are for that moment when you decide you want a decadent dessert ASAP. They can be filled with anything from fresh fruit to peanut butter. I like them stuffed with dark chocolate like this, but feel free to mix and match your fillings.

4 slices of brioche bread (normal white bread will do if you don't have brioche)
2 tablespoons salted butter
50 g (1¾ oz) dark chocolate, roughly chopped
1 tablespoon caster sugar

For the custard
2 eggs
2 tablespoons caster sugar
1 teaspoon vanilla extract
50 ml (2 fl oz) milk
50 ml (2 fl oz) double cream
pinch of sea salt

To serve
icing sugar
ice cream, or crème fraîche

1 > In a jug or bowl, whisk together the ingredients for the custard and set aside until needed.

2 > Take 2 of the brioche slices and butter them well. Divide the chopped chocolate between them, placing it in the centre of each slice, with a 1.5 cm (⅝ inch) border. Place the other 2 brioche slices on top, pressing them down to seal around the edges and encase the chocolate centres.

3> Melt the remaining butter in a large non-stick frying pan over a medium–high heat. While the butter is melting, tip half the custard onto a plate and dip one of the brioche parcels in it, turning it as you do so. You want it to be coated and soaked, but don't leave it in there longer than 45 seconds or it'll start to disintegrate!

4 > Transfer the custard-coated parcel to the hot pan, then quickly repeat the process with the remaining custard and parcel. Fry the parcels for 2 minutes. Use a spatula to press down on them a little, then scatter some caster sugar over the top of each one: this will create a nice, crunchy caramel surface when you fry this side. Use the spatula to flip the parcels over, pressing them down again and cooking for 1 minute or so, until crisp and golden on the underside.

5 > Transfer the parcels to 2 plates, dust with icing sugar and slice in half, revealing the melty chocolate centre. Serve with ice cream or crème fraîche.

COCONUT AND PINEAPPLE 'CRÊPES SUZETTE'

This is a bit more fiddly than some of the other desserts, but you can make everything in advance and reheat in the pan when you want to serve.

1 small pineapple
1 tablespoon coconut, sunflower
  or vegetable oil
6 tablespoons dark brown sugar
200 ml (7 fl oz) coconut milk
pinch of sea salt
75 ml (2½ fl oz) whisky or
  bourbon

For the crêpe batter
100 g (3½ oz) plain flour
pinch of sea salt
2 eggs
200 ml (7 fl oz) coconut milk
coconut, sunflower or vegetable
  oil, for frying

To serve
ice cream
toasted coconut flakes

1 > Start by making the crêpe batter. In a large bowl, mix together the flour and salt. Create a hole in the centre and crack the eggs into it. Pour in the coconut milk and 130 ml (4½ fl oz) water. Whisk to create a batter with the consistency of double cream, adding a splash more water if you need to. Rest in the refrigerator while you prepare the pineapple.

2 > Cut the spiky top off the pineapple and carefully slice down the sides to cut away the skin. Slice in half lengthways, then slice into half-moons around 5 mm (¼ inch) thick. Set aside on a board or plate.

3 > To make the crêpes, heat 1 teaspoon oil in a large non-stick frying pan over a medium–high heat. (I use kitchen roll to spread the oil evenly across the pan.) Add a ladleful of batter and swirl the pan so the batter thinly covers the base. Cook for 1 minute, then flip and cook for a further 30 seconds. Set aside on a plate. Repeat with the rest of the batter, adding a little more oil as you go to stop them from sticking. Don't worry if you lose a couple of crêpes at the start: you should still get 8. Pile the pancakes on top of each other on the plate and set aside.

4 > Keep the pan on the heat and add 1 tablespoon oil. Once hot, add the pineapple slices and fry for 5–10 minutes, until caramelized. Set the pineapple aside, then sprinkle the sugar into the pan. Pour in the coconut milk. Stir gently and bring to the boil. Add a pinch of salt and cook for 2 minutes, until you are left with a syrupy sauce. (You can now cover everything and set it aside in the refrigerator to assemble later.)

5 > Add the whisky to the pan and toss, then reduce the heat to low. Fold the crêpes into triangles and nestle them into the sauce. Heat for a few minutes to warm through. Add the pineapple to reheat, if you like.

6 > To serve, place 2 folded crêpes on each plate, top with the pineapple and drizzle with the remaining sauce from the pan. Serve with ice cream and toasted coconut flakes.

POACHED PEACHES
WITH CRÈME FRAÎCHE AND TOASTED HAZELNUTS

This is a super simple and elegant dessert. You can use the same method to poach plums or nectarines, depending on what you can get hold of.

50 g (1¾ oz) hazelnuts
250 ml (9 fl oz) dry white or rosé
   wine
4 ripe peaches, halved and stoned
120 g (4¼ oz) golden caster sugar
1 teaspoon vanilla extract
4 tablespoons crème fraîche,
   to serve

1 > Heat a large saucepan over a medium heat. Add the hazelnuts and toast for around 5 minutes, shaking the pan constantly so they become evenly brown. Tip on to a chopping board and leave to cool.

2 > Tip the wine into the pan, along with 200 ml (7 fl oz) water, and bring to the boil. Reduce the heat to a simmer, add the peach halves and poach for 10–15 minutes, until soft. Use a slotted spoon to remove the peaches and transfer them to a plate.

3 > Add the sugar and vanilla extract to the pan and increase the heat to high. Boil for 12–15 minutes, until the sauce has reduced by half and you are left with a syrupy mixture.

4 > Meanwhile, roughly chop the hazelnuts and peel the peaches. (You can leave the skin on the peaches if you prefer, but they're easier to eat if the skin is removed.)

5 > Return the peaches to the pan and gently toss in the syrupy sauce, then spoon into 4 bowls. To serve, top with a dollop of crème fraîche and scatter over the chopped hazelnuts.

PB AND J CRUMBLE

Peanut butter is my favourite thing in the world, which makes this crumble basically the best crumble I've eaten. You can make it in the winter with frozen berries or in the summer with fresh berries. Serve it warm like a traditional crumble or leave it to cool and then serve it in tall glasses with ice cream, like an ice cream sundae with all the good stuff. To make this suitable for vegans, serve with dairy-free custard or ice cream.

For the topping

60 g (2¼ oz) salted butter

3 tablespoons crunchy peanut butter

4 tablespoons golden or maple syrup

100 g (3½ oz) self-raising flour

70 g (2½ oz) jumbo oats

3 tablespoons roasted, salted peanuts, roughly chopped (optional)

pinch of sea salt

custard or ice cream, to serve

For the filling

800 g (1 lb 12 oz) mixed berries (I like to use strawberries and raspberries)

80 g (2¾ oz) caster sugar

1 teaspoon vanilla essence

zest and juice of 1 unwaxed lemon

1 > Melt the butter, peanut butter and syrup in a large non-stick frying pan over a low heat. Whisk to combine. Mix together the remaining topping ingredients in a large bowl. Tip this mixture into the pan and stir to coat: it should clump a little in places. Toast over the low heat for 15–20 minutes, until crisp and golden. Stir and shake the pan regularly to stop it catching on the base of the pan.

2 > Meanwhile, place the berries in a large bowl, slicing any that are too big. Add the sugar, vanilla essence and lemon zest and mix together.

3 > Once the crumble topping is cooked through, tip it on to a plate or into a bowl and set aside. Return the pan to a medium heat and add the berry mixture. Stir well, then cover with a lid and cook for 10 minutes.

4 > Remove the lid and add the lemon juice, then simmer gently for 8–10 minutes further, until thickened and jammy.

5 > Remove from the heat and top with the crumble topping. Serve warm with custard or ice cream, or let it cool and make it into an ice cream sundae.

A KIND OF BANOFFEE PUDDING

Piling the biscuits on top of the banana base means they stay crunchy without needing to be chilled – the ultimate trick to completely avoiding a soggy-based dessert. This method also means that if you, like me, hate waiting for your favourite desserts to cool, you can just enjoy it warm with ice cream.

60 g (2¼ oz) unsalted butter
4 large ripe bananas, peeled and
  each cut into 4 chunky slices on
  an angle
50 g (1¾ oz) dark brown sugar
200 g (7 oz) can condensed milk
1 teaspoon vanilla extract
pinch of sea salt
4 tablespoons double cream
150 g (5½ oz) digestive biscuits,
  roughly broken up
whipped (or squirty) cream or ice
  cream, to serve

1 > Heat half the butter in a large non-stick frying pan over a high heat. Once the butter is foaming, add the banana slices and fry for 2–3 minutes until caramelized. Remove and set aside on a plate. You might have to do this in 2 batches.

2 > Reduce the heat to medium and add the remaining butter to the pan. Sprinkle in the sugar and stir until melted. Pour the condensed milk into the pan, along with the vanilla extract and salt. Cook for 8–10 minutes, stirring regularly so it doesn't catch, until the sauce is dark-caramel coloured and very thick. Add the double cream to loosen the sauce, then remove the pan from the heat and set aside to cool a little. Return the bananas to the pan, gently coating them in the caramel sauce.

3 > Top the pan with the broken-up digestives. At this point, you can let it cool completely, before serving covered with whipped cream, or, if you want to eat it straight away, spoon it into 6 bowls and serve with scoops of ice cream.

Photograph overleaf >

KEY LIME PIE-ISH

This does require a little refrigerator time, but it takes 5 minutes to make and it tastes like you've spent hours following the detailed instructions of a patisserie book! Rather than serving it in individual bowls, it works just as well if you want to double the recipe and set it in a big serving dish to plonk in the middle of the table.

300 ml (10 fl oz) double cream
3 tablespoons golden caster
   sugar
juice of 3 limes
pinch of sea salt

To serve
zest of 1 unwaxed lime
gingernut biscuits

1 > Tip 200 ml (7 fl oz) of the double cream into a large saucepan over a medium heat. Add the caster sugar and bring to the boil, stirring constantly. Once boiling, set a timer for 2½ minutes. Boil vigorously until the timer goes off, stirring as it counts down. Remove from the heat and allow the mixture to relax for a minute or two, then stir in the lime juice and salt.

2 > Pour the mixture into a serving dish and cover with a sheet of clingfilm, pressing it down to touch the surface of the cream mixture: this will stop the cream developing a skin. Set aside in the refrigerator for a couple of hours.

3 > To serve, whip up the remaining double cream until it has soft, silky peaks. Use a spatula or spoon to fold half the whipped cream through the set cream: this will loosen and lighten it. Spoon the creamy mixture into 4 bowls and top with a dollop of the remaining whipped cream. Zest the lime over the top and serve with the gingernut biscuits for dunking.

BABY SPICED DOUGHNUTS

These little guys are the easiest, quickest doughnuts I've ever made. Based on a dessert that I love at Ducksoup restaurant in London, the doughnuts are kind of shallow-fried. I like dipping them in custard or serving them with a dollop of crème fraîche. (I also like eating them straight after rolling them in the sugar!)

250 g (9 oz) ricotta, drained
2 eggs
140 g (5 oz) plain flour
4 teaspoons baking powder
225 g (8 oz) caster sugar
pinch of sea salt
1 teaspoon ground cinnamon
1 teaspoon ground ginger
sunflower or vegetable oil, for
frying
custard or crème fraîche, to serve
(optional)

1 > In a mixing bowl, whisk together the ricotta and the eggs. Add the flour and baking powder, along with 1 tablespoon of the caster sugar and the salt. Whisk again to combine.

2 > Tip the remaining caster sugar into a separate bowl. Add the cinnamon and ginger and stir to combine. Set aside until needed.

3 > Take a large high-sided frying pan and pour in enough oil to come about 3 cm (1¼ inch) up the side of the pan. Place over a high heat. It'll take 3–5 minutes to heat up to the right temperature. While you're waiting, line a plate with kitchen paper.

4 > To test the oil, turn the heat down to medium–low and drop a tiny pinch of the batter – about half a teaspoon – into the oil. It should bubble immediately and cook through in a minute. If the oil is too cool, increase the heat for a minute or so longer. If it's too hot and the dough bubbles vigorously as it quickly turns dark brown, remove from the heat and either add a glug of cold oil, or allow to cool for 5 minutes, then try again.

5 > When you're ready to fry, take a teaspoon of the batter and use a second teaspoon to slide it into the oil. Cook for 1½–2 minutes, until the batter turns into a little doughnut, golden and puffed up, then use a spatula to flip it over. Cook the other side for 2 minutes, then use a slotted spoon to transfer the doughnut to the lined plate to drain off any excess oil. Repeat with the rest of the batter, cooking several at a time, stopping every now and then to toss the warm, drained doughnuts in the bowl of spiced sugar.

6 > Serve as soon as possible, while still warm, with custard or crème fraîche if you like.

APPLE HAND PIES

This recipe started out as a big apple filo pie, but then I realized that it would work so much better as individual hand pies – you get extra-crispy filo pastry encasing the caramel apple filling and you don't have to worry about anyone getting a larger slice than you!

100 g (3½ oz) salted butter
60 g (2¼ oz) golden caster sugar
4 apples, quartered, cored and
    cut into 2 cm (¾ inch) chunks
    (no need to peel)
1 teaspoon ground cinnamon
60 g (2¼ oz) toasted flaked
    almonds
pinch of sea salt
4 sheets ready-made filo pastry

To serve
icing sugar
crème fraîche (optional)

1 > Melt 60 g (2¼ oz) of the butter in a large non-stick frying pan over a medium heat. Add the sugar to the pan, along with the apple chunks and cinnamon. Allow to bubble for 8–10 minutes, stirring regularly, until the apples are soft. Add the almonds and salt and cook for 3 more minutes, then tip into a bowl and set aside to cool for 5 minutes. Wipe out the pan.

2 > Lay out a sheet of filo on the work surface and fold one side over the other, like a book, creating a square of around 25 cm (10 inches). Add a dollop of about one-quarter of the apple filling to the middle of the bottom third of one of the pastry squares and shape the filling into a 10 cm (4 inch) horizontal sausage shape. Fold the bottom of the pastry over the filling, then fold the sides over the top. Roll the pastry up from the bottom to create a sausage-shaped parcel. Use a little water to seal it together at the top. Repeat with the remaining filo pastry sheets and apple mixture to create 4 parcels.

3 > Melt the remaining butter in the pan over a low–medium heat, then add 2 of the apple parcels. Press down a little with the back of a spoon or spatula, and fry for 2–3 minutes on each side until golden, crisp and cooked all the way through. Make sure the heat is not too high, or the pies will get too golden before the filling is cooked. Set aside and repeat with the other 2 parcels. Dust with icing sugar and serve, preferably with crème fraîche for dipping!

GLOSSARY OF UK/US INGREDIENTS

Ingredients

aubergine – **eggplant**
beef fillet – **beef tenderloin**
beef mince – **ground beef**
beetroot – **beet**
borlotti beans – **cranberry beans**
broad beans – **fava beans**
butter beans – **lima beans**
cannellini beans – **white kidney beans**
caster sugar – **superfine sugar**
chickpeas – **garbanzo beans**
cider – **hard cider**
cornflour – **corn starch**
coriander (fresh) – **cilantro**
digestive biscuits – **graham crackers**
double cream – **heavy cream**
giant couscous – **Israeli couscous**
gingernut biscuits – **ginger snap cookies**
icing sugar – **confectioners' sugar/powdered sugar**
jumbo oats – **whole rolled oats**
king prawns – **jumbo shrimp**
lamb mince – **ground lamb**
long-stem broccoli – **broccolini**

natural yogurt – **plain yogurt**
pak choi – **bok choy**
passata – **sieved tomatoes (sometimes sold as tomato puree in the US)**
peppers (red/green/yellow) – **bell peppers**
plain flour – **all-purpose flour**
pork mince – **ground pork**
prawns – **shrimp**
rolled oats – **old-fashioned rolled oats**
self-raising flour – **self-rising flour**
soured cream – **sour cream**
spring onions – **scallions**
stock – **broth**
sultanas – **golden raisins**
tomato puree – **tomato paste**

Equipment

baking paper – **parchment paper**
fish slice – **slotted spatula**
frying pan – **skillet**
kitchen roll – **paper towels**
grill – **broiler**
tea towel – **dish towel**
tin foil – **aluminum foil**

INDEX

ACKNOWLEDGEMENTS

A big thank you to my whole lockdown family bubble, for doing endless washing up and tasting countless dishes during the weeks we were all in the house together – my parents, Annie and Charlie, and my constantly hungry brother Harry and his girlfriend, Georgia. You guys made this process a whole lot easier and so much fun.

To everyone who worked on the shoot and made the recipes look so delicious – the ridiculously talented Louise Hagger, Alexander Breeze, Sophie Bronze, Sonali Shah and Benjamina Ebuehi. You were an absolute joy to work with.

To Sophie Godwin, for reading, correcting, testing and generally making me better at my job than I would be otherwise.

To my incredible pals that tested and tasted recipes from afar – Anna Lawson, Joe Crossley, Chloe King, Abi James, Sophie Mcdowell, Suzy Dansie, Faye Scott-Maberley, Sherri Dymond and Bella Haycroft-Mee. Your feedback and support made this book better.

To all the team at Octopus – my fantastic commissioning editor Louise McKeever, Alex Stetter, Caroline Alberti and Yasia Williams. Thank you for giving me the opportunity to write this book and for making it look so fab.